To All on Equal Terms

The Life and Legacy of Prudence Crandall

Research and Text by
Diana Ross McCain

Design by
Laura Butler
Angell House Design

In Collaboration with
Kazimiera Kozlowski
Curator • Prudence Crandall Museum

SPONSORS

State of Connecticut
John G. Rowland • Governor

Connecticut Commission on Arts, Tourism, Culture, History and Film
Jennifer Aniskovich • Executive Director

Historic Preservation and Museum Division
J. Paul Loether • Acting Director, Deputy State Historic Preservation Officer

2004

Commission on Arts, Tourism, Culture, History and Film

Sid Beighley	Bruce Fraser*	Marilyn Nelson*
Nicholas Bellantoni*	*Ex. Director of CT Humanities Council*	*State Poet Laureate*
State Archaeologist	Steven Gardiner	Michael P. Price, Chair
Charles F. Bunnell	Adam Grabinski	Linda H. Roth
Carolyn F. Cicchetti, Vice Chair	Astrid Hanzalek	Clement J. Roy
Christopher Collier*	Helen Higgins*	Rita M. Schmidt
State Historian	*Ex. Director of CT Trust for Historic Preservation*	William Schwab
Jack Condlin		Ann Elizabeth Sheffer
Arthur Diedrick	Harvey Hubbell	Douglas H. Teeson
Angelo Faenza	Fritz Jellinghaus	Ted Yudain
Henry Fernandez	Michael R. Kintner	
Walter M. Fiederowicz	Lawrence D. McHugh	** Ex-Officio Members*

© Connecticut Commission on Arts, Tourism, Culture, History and Film. All rights reserved.
No part of this report may be reproduced or transmitted in any form or by any means, electronic or mechanical, including photocopying, recording, or by any information storage and retrieval system without permission in writing from the Connecticut Commission on Arts, Tourism, Culture, History and Film, One Financial Plaza, 755 Main Street, Hartford, CT 06103.

Additional copies may be obtained from the
Prudence Crandall Museum
P.O. Box 58
Routes 14 and 169, Canterbury, CT 06331
(860) 546-7800

Funding for this project was made available in part by the Connecticut General Assembly through the Connecticut State Library under Public Act 02-7, Sec. 108 - Grants to Local Institutions in the Humanities.

"I contemplated for a while the manner in which I might best serve the people of color. As wealth was not mine, I saw no other means of benefitting them, than by imparting to those of my own sex that were anxious to learn, all the instruction I might be able to give, however small the amount."

Prudence Crandall, *Windham County Herald*, May 7, 1833

"... it is doubtful that any child may reasonably be expected to succeed in life if he is denied the opportunity of an education. Such an opportunity, where the state has undertaken to provide it, is a right which must be made available to all on equal terms."

From the Opinion of the United States Supreme Court on Brown v. Board of Education, 1954, delivered by Chief Justice Earl Warren

ACKNOWLEDGEMENTS

Many people and institutions – far too many to list individually – played a role in making this publication a reality. However, the involvement of three historians in this three-year undertaking was so essential that they must be thanked by name.

Connecticut State Historian **Christopher "Kit" Collier** generously granted access to his extensive files of research on Prudence Crandall and many related topics. He also provided encouragement, advice, and direction based on his deep knowledge and thought about the state's past, and offered his informed, insightful, critical comments on the finished manuscript and the design.

David O. White, who was the first curator of the Prudence Crandall Museum, critiqued the manuscript from his vast knowledge of the Prudence Crandall story and knowledge of the history of African Americans in nineteenth-century Connecticut.

Robert P. Forbes, associate director of the Gilder Lehrman Center for the Study of Slavery, Resistance, and Abolition at the Yale Center for International and Area Studies, read the manuscript and made valuable comments.

INTRODUCTION

The Connecticut Commission on Arts, Tourism, Culture, History and Film is pleased to publish *To All On Equal Terms: The Life and Legacy of Prudence Crandall* in celebration of the Prudence Crandall Museum's twentieth anniversary, and in recognition of the fiftieth anniversary of the 1954 landmark U.S. Supreme Court school desegregation decision Brown v. Board of Education of Topeka.

Through the efforts of preservationists, historians, civic-minded individuals, and state officials, one of Connecticut's greatest treasures was saved from the wrecking ball, purchased by the State of Connecticut in 1969, and formally dedicated as a museum in 1984. The words Governor William O'Neill spoke on May 18, 1984 at the museum's dedication are just as relevant today.

> *"…I suppose there are some people around our state who might ask – why should we preserve buildings like the Prudence Crandall House? Aren't there other things on which we should spend our money?*
>
> *I believe the answer is – yes there are many things on which public funds can be spent, and the preservation of our heritage is certainly an important item on that agenda. I am sure that those doubting Thomases believe in educating our young people to be the leaders of tomorrow. Well, part of that education involves an understanding of how we got where we are, so that we will be better able to decide how to go on from here. Clearly, the Prudence Crandall House contributes to that understanding…*
>
> *Yes, there is much to learn within these walls, about the courage and commitment of our ancestors, about the early struggle to achieve equal rights…it is all right here, within these walls, and – yes – it is very much worth saving. The lessons to be learned here are lessons for a lifetime, not just our lifetime, but lifetimes of generations yet unborn.*
>
> *As one of the original 13 colonies, Connecticut certainly is secure in its place in American history, and – beginning today – the Prudence Crandall House is certainly secure in its place in the history of Connecticut."*

Since that day in 1984, thousands of visitors from near and far have passed through the doors of the Prudence Crandall Museum. Why do they come? Because the physical relics of the past have the power to make history come alive. They connect us, both intellectually and emotionally, to the lives and stories of generations past.

It is my hope that *To All On Equal Terms* will serve to educate, enlighten, and, most importantly, inspire you, the reader. After the closing of Prudence Crandall's academy in 1834, more than 120 years would pass before the Brown v. Board of Education decision decreed an end to segregation in the nation's public schools. But the fundamental lesson of both events is the same: in each case, individuals displayed the courage to act on the belief that society's opportunities must be made available to all on equal terms.

Jennifer Aniskovich, Executive Director
Connecticut Commission on Arts, Tourism, Culture, History and Film
2004

FOREWORD

In law, as in education and civil rights, Prudence Crandall left a powerful and enduring legacy.

Crandall's decision to open an academy for black women defied contemporary social norms — and state law. In 1833, Crandall was tried and convicted of violating a state statue that prohibited the unlicensed instruction of non-resident "colored" persons.

Crandall appealed her conviction to the Supreme Court of Errors, then the state's highest court. It overturned her conviction, but on a technicality. The judges never ruled on Crandall's unprecedented claim that the U.S. Constitution prohibited state-sanctioned discrimination — contended for the first time in an American courtroom.

In the coming years, Crandall's case provided ammunition in the struggle for civil rights. In 1857, pro-slavery lawyers cited Crandall's original conviction in the Dred Scott case, helping to persuade the U.S. Supreme Court to rule that African-Americans had no rights under the U.S. Constitution. The court's decision hastened the Civil War.

Almost 100 years later, civil rights lawyers applied Crandall's powerful arguments in Brown v. Board of Education, successfully fighting to strike down public school segregation. They called her appeal "one of the classic statements of the social and ethical case for equality of opportunity irrespective of race," and the "first comprehensive crystallization of antislavery constitutional theory."

Through her courage and conviction — and her simple desire to educate all regardless of race — Crandall helped create landmark constitutional principles that eventually became the law of the land.

> Richard Blumenthal
> Attorney General
> State of Connecticut

Prudence Crandall's humane and egalitarian instincts found material expression in the alteration of her school from a place for upper-class girls to get an advanced education, to a school for the same purposes for African-American girls only. Her cause was quickly embraced by abolitionists and other friends of black Americans who were looking for a case that would test Article IV, Section 2, paragraph 1 of the U.S. Constitution: "The Citizens of each State shall be entitled to all the Privileges and Immunities of Citizens in the several States." The constitutional question was: are free African Americans in free states citizens?

Unfortunately, the highest Connecticut court chose to dodge the question by invoking a legalistic technicality. The reasoning of the prosecution – which was not part of the court's finding – was used to uphold the majority opinion in the U. S. Supreme Court's decision in Dred Scott v. Sanford in 1857: black Americans were not and could not be citizens.

The Crandall episode was, however, of great political significance in Connecticut. It helped turn around public opinion in regard to the rights of Africans and African Americans and make what had the reputation as the most racist state in the North into one in which abolitionist sentiment was allowed to develop and flower. This was of great significance six years after Prudence was driven from Canterbury, when her principal tormentor, Andrew Judson, as a U. S. District judge, had to decide the fate of the *Amistad* captives. He felt the force of public opinion and in an extraordinary change of heart, freed the kidnapped Africans who had seized the ship carrying them to slavery.

The Civil Rights movement of the 1960s reawakened Connecticut citizens' recognition of Crandall's courageous stand. That stand that has inspired hundreds of teachers and others to make her cause theirs.

> Dr. Christopher Collier
> Connecticut State Historian

TABLE OF CONTENTS

PROLOGUE	1
CHAPTER ONE • Shake-Up in the Land of Steady Habits: Connecticut and Canterbury in the 1830s	2
CHAPTER TWO • Rebellion in the Blood: Prudence Crandall and the Crandall Family	6
CHAPTER THREE • Only Three R's – Except for the Rich: Public and Private Education in Early Nineteenth-Century Connecticut	8
CHAPTER FOUR • A Golden Opportunity: The Canterbury Female Boarding School, 1831-2	10
CHAPTER FIVE • "To Get A Little More Learning": A Student of Color Seeks Admission	13
CHAPTER SIX • No Small Courage: Two Women Stand Up for the Right to an Education	15
CHAPTER SEVEN • "Truly This Is Our Home": The History of Connecticut's Black Community	16
CHAPTER EIGHT • The Voice of Conscience Grows Louder: Searching for Solutions to Slavery and Racism	22
CHAPTER NINE • Seizing the Sword of Truth: Prudence Crandall Confounds Her Critics	25
CHAPTER TEN • Raging Bullies: The Battle of Canterbury Begins	27
CHAPTER ELEVEN • Adding Prosecution to Persecution: Using Old and New Laws to Close the Canterbury Female Boarding School	30
CHAPTER TWELVE • When All Else Failed: Turning to the Tactics of Terror	39
CHAPTER THIRTEEN • In The Whirlwind's Wake: Exile, Tribulation, and Vindication	41
CHAPTER FOURTEEN • "To All On Equal Terms": The Legacy of Prudence Crandall and the Canterbury Female Boarding School	48
CHAPTER FIFTEEN • Sites in Eastern Connecticut Associated with the Prudence Crandall Episode	50
ILLUSTRATION IDENTIFICATION AND CREDITS/SELECTED BIBLIOGRAPHY	52

PROLOGUE

In Canterbury, Connecticut, in the spring of 1833, Miss Prudence Crandall opened a private school for "young Ladies and little Misses of color." African-American girls from Boston, New York City, Philadelphia, Providence, and several Connecticut towns enrolled in the Canterbury Female Boarding School, located in Prudence Crandall's handsome, spacious house on the village green. They studied subjects including reading, writing, arithmetic, grammar, geography, history, chemistry, astronomy, and French.

Even before it opened, Prudence Crandall's school aroused fear, anger, even hatred in many Canterbury residents. The school quickly became the flash point for a controversy that rapidly flared into a crisis involving leading figures in politics, law, civil rights, and religion that drew much international attention.

The Connecticut General Assembly passed legislation for the specific purpose of closing the Canterbury Female Boarding School. Prudence Crandall was then arrested, jailed, and tried three times for violating that law. Many Canterbury merchants, as well as a local doctor and minister, shunned Prudence and her black students. Vandals polluted her well, smashed her windows with rocks, and at one point tried to burn down her house.

Finally, on the night of September 9, 1834, a mob attacked the house, while Prudence and 20 students were inside. The crowd pounded the building with wooden and metal clubs, ripped out windows, and ransacked the first floor. Prudence and her students feared for their lives. The next day Prudence sent her students home and closed the Canterbury Female Boarding School for good.

Why did the Canterbury Female Boarding School ignite a firestorm of such violent fury?
And why, 170 years later, does its story still matter?

CHAPTER ONE

Shake-up In The Land of Steady Habits

CONNECTICUT AND CANTERBURY IN THE 1830s

In the 1830s, Connecticut, nicknamed the "Land of Steady Habits" for its stable and conservative ways, was in the throes of a profoundly unsettling transformation. Traditions, institutions, and practices that had shaped politics, culture, economy, and community and family life for 200 years were changing. These rapid and radical turns left many Connecticut residents uneasy and suspicious of any changes that might further upset their lives.

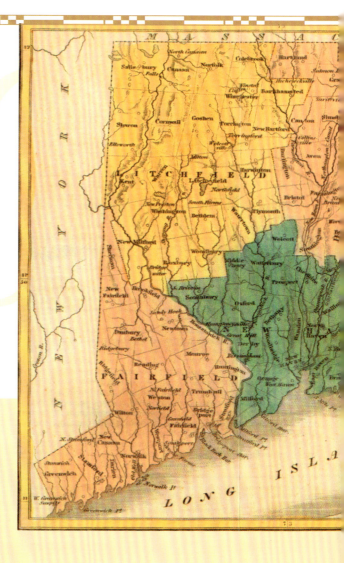

ECONOMY

Most Connecticut families farmed for a living. But as the population exploded during the 1700s, demand for land grew fierce, and prices skyrocketed. Many acres, not very fertile to start with, had been depleted by decades of cultivation. It became more difficult to support a family by tilling Connecticut's expensive, overworked soil. Interest grew in fresh, cheap land on frontiers like that in northeastern Ohio advertised for sale in 1817 in the *Connecticut Courant*, shown at left.

Beginning in the 1700s, towns on Long Island Sound and on major rivers such as the Connecticut and the Thames carried on profitable maritime trade with ports in the West Indies, along the Atlantic seaboard, and in Europe. But by 1830 the state's seafaring heyday was over. It had been destroyed by embargoes on foreign commerce imposed by the federal government between 1807 and 1810, and by the British enemy's blockade of American ports during the War of 1812. The impact upon thousands of people who depended upon the maritime trade for their livelihood was devastating.

RELIGION

Religion, the single most powerful force in Connecticut from its founding, was also changing profoundly. Since the mid-1600s Congregationalism had been Connecticut's established, state-supported church. Until the 1790s, all other faiths were strongly discouraged by law and popular opinion. Congregationalism's special status gave it great influence in government and public education, and it was intimately tied to the conservative Federalist party, which dominated Connecticut politics following the American Revolution.

By the early 1800s new religious denominations had taken root in Connecticut. By 1836 in Bridgeport, for example, the houses of worship of four different denominations stood a short distance from each other: Episcopalian, Congregational, Baptist, and Methodist.

Episcopalians, Baptists, and Methodists joined other opponents of the Congregationalists/Federalists to form the Tolerationist Party, which in 1817 elected Oliver Wolcott, Jr., governor. The next year a new state constitution stripped the Congregational church of the special privileges it had enjoyed for nearly two centuries.

Governor Oliver Wolcott, Jr.

"We saw fighting side by side, shoulder to shoulder, democracy, Methodism, Episcopacy, Pedobaptism, Universalism, radicalism, infidelity – all united for the overthrow of federalism and orthodoxy."
— Samuel Griswold Goodrich, *Recollections of a Lifetime*, 1856

EXODUS

Connecticut's more adventurous, ambitious, restless, or desperate sons and daughters, seeking better economic opportunities or a less oppressive religious and political climate, had been leaving the state by the thousands since the 1760s. That exodus accelerated in the early 1800s. A common sight on Connecticut roads was a family in a wagon packed with all their worldly goods heading out of the state.

The emigrants' quest took them hundreds of miles from home, to Vermont, Ohio, Pennsylvania, New York State, and sometimes to even more distant destinations, such as Georgia. Few ever returned permanently to Connecticut.

"Ohio – with its rich soil, its mild climate, its inviting prairies – was opened fully . . . a sort of stampede took place from cold, desolate, worn-out New England, to this land of promise."
— Samuel Griswold Goodrich, *Recollections of a Lifetime*, 1856

This mania for migrating stunted Connecticut's population growth. It siphoned off some of the state's best and brightest young people, disrupting families and entire communities. The article at right from the *Connecticut Courant* in 1817 bemoaned the flood of panicked emigrants.

Between 1820 and 1830, the United States' population skyrocketed by one third, from 9,638,000 to 12,866,00. During that same period Connecticut's population increased just eight percent, from 275,248 to 297,675. Canterbury's population actually *declined* by five percent during this period.

A deplorable species of madness.—It is said by some who lately have travelled the great roads in which are the principal streams of emigration from East to West, and have enquired of innkeepers on the subject, that the numbers emigrating have been far greater this year than at any former period; also, that many of them had not fixed before hand on any particular place for their future residence. One gentleman, a man of high respectability, informed us that he met a long line of teams, thirty in number, and asking the drivers, one by one, whither they were bound, almost all of them replied, "We are bound to the Westward," seeming not to know themselves, what particular spot, or town, or district of the "vasty" West would terminate their migrations.

Many professionals could still make a respectable living in Connecticut, and thus had less incentive to emigrate. Individuals who were comfortable with the state's still-conservative political and religious atmosphere were also less likely to leave. A number of such men lived in handsome houses in the center of Canterbury, like the one shown above. They included attorneys Daniel Frost, Jr., Rufus Adams, and Andrew Judson; Dr. Andrew Harris; merchants Stephen Coit, Luther Paine, Ebenezer Sanger, and Samuel Hough; and factory owner Gad Buckley. They and their families enjoyed an active, cultured social life.

Manufacturing, which would prove to be Connecticut's economic salvation, was in its very early stages. In 1836 Killingly was Connecticut's largest cotton manufacturing town. It boasted 14 mills, including the four-story factory with a tower just left of the center in the village of Danielsonville. Nearby Canterbury boasted only three cotton mills.

CHAPTER TWO
Rebellion in the Blood
PRUDENCE CRANDALL AND THE CRANDALL FAMILY

Prudence Crandall came from a heritage of stubborn non-conformists. Her parents were Quakers, members of a faith that comprised a tiny minority of New England residents in the 1830s. When Quakers first arrived in Massachusetts in the 1600s, they were persecuted and even executed for their beliefs. By the mid-1700s, Quakers were committed to peace, tolerance, and the equality of men and women and of members of all races.

Prudence received the basics of education in a Quaker school on Black Hill in Canterbury. She also acquired the traditional feminine skills such as sewing, which she demonstrated by stitching the sampler shown at left.

The Crandall Family

Esther Carpenter and Pardon Crandall married in 1799 in Hopkinton, Rhode Island, where three children were born to them: Hezekiah in 1800, Prudence in 1803, and Reuben in 1806. Their fourth and final child, a daughter named Almira, was born shortly after they moved to Canterbury in 1813.

Mother

Father

Pardon Crandall bought one of the largest farms in Canterbury, and by the early 1830s was one of the town's most prosperous residents. Pardon and Esther Crandall made formal education a high priority for their children. Son Reuben attended college, while both Prudence and Almira received a far more advanced education than most women of their era.

At the age of 22 Prudence enrolled in the academically excellent New England Yearly Meeting School in Providence, Rhode Island. This was a Quaker institution, founded by Moses Brown, a wealthy Quaker who freed his slaves and became an active advocate of the abolition of slavery. The years Prudence studied there reinforced the anti-slavery principles with which she had grown up. Almira Crandall also attended the New England Yearly Meeting School.

"[I was] taught from early childhood the sin of Slavery…"
— Prudence Crandall to Ellen Larned, May 15, 1869

By the end of the American Revolution, New England Quakers condemned enslavement of blacks as a crime against fellow human beings. That conviction was expressed in the widely reproduced image of a slave in chains proclaiming his humanity.

In 1830, Prudence was 27 — well past the age at which New England women typically wed. She seems to have had no plans or prospects for marriage. Her goal was to be an independent, self-supporting woman. She became a teacher at a private school in the nearby town of Plainfield, shown in the engraving below.

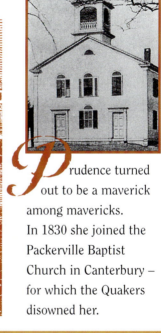

Prudence turned out to be a maverick among mavericks. In 1830 she joined the Packerville Baptist Church in Canterbury – for which the Quakers disowned her.

Brother
The eldest Crandall child, Hezekiah, didn't pursue higher education, but went directly into business. In 1829 he purchased a cotton mill in Canterbury.

Brother
Reuben Crandall received his diploma, at right, from Yale in 1828. After serving an apprenticeship under Dr. Andrew Harris of Canterbury, Reuben opened a medical practice in Peekskill, New York.

CHAPTER THREE

Only Three R's – Except for the Rich
PUBLIC AND PRIVATE EDUCATION IN EARLY NINETEENTH-CENTURY CONNECTICUT

Beginning in 1650, Connecticut required towns to establish schools to teach children to read and write, so they could have "knowledge of the scriptures" – the Bible, which was the foundation of the Puritan settlers' faith. But there was little support for education beyond basic literacy, and perhaps simple arithmetic, which in the early 1800s many people still considered all the book learning a man or woman needed for daily life. Taxpayers spent as little as they could get away with on the public or "common" schools. Students' parents often were required to make contributions beyond their regular taxes.

PUBLIC EDUCATION

Common schools were typically hastily built, poorly maintained one-room structures that were badly lit and ventilated, freezing cold in winter and stiflingly hot in summer. Many common schools didn't even have outhouses for students to use.

Furnishings and supplies were scarce and often crude. Students sat on rough benches made of split logs, and wrote their lessons on slates, for paper was very expensive. There were no learning tools such as blackboards or maps.

Forty or more children, as young as four or as old as eighteen, might be crowded into a schoolhouse like the one shown above, with one teacher responsible for educating all of them.

Teaching was not a skilled, respected profession, but a temporary, poorly paid, low-prestige job. There were no training standards for teachers, who at times were younger than some of their students. Maintaining discipline was a major challenge; some teachers resorted to beating, humiliating, or shutting children up in closets to control them.

"Bishop was our first teacher – a poor creature who didn't know what else to do, so he kept school." — Lyman Beecher, *Autobiography*, 1865

PRIVATE EDUCATION

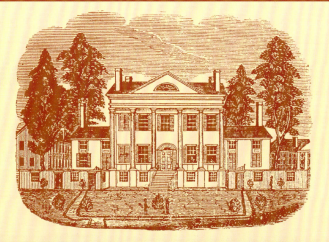

During the first decades of the 1800s, a growing number of parents were dissatisfied with the limited, mediocre education offered by the common schools. This led to the establishment of many private academies for boys in Connecticut. These schools offered an alternative to the common school for parents who didn't need their children's labor to make ends meet and who could afford the tuition. Pupils at these schools, which attracted many out-of-state students, studied advanced subjects in a variety of disciplines.

Private schools that instructed daughters of the well-to-do in needlework and painting had existed in New England since before the Revolution. But in the early 1800s there began to appear private girls' schools that taught the same subjects as boys' academies. Typically these were run by an unmarried woman or a widow who needed to support herself. One of the country's best private girls' schools was the Hartford Female Seminary, established by Catharine Beecher, sister of Harriet Beecher Stowe.

Attendance was not mandatory, and many children went to school irregularly – or not at all. Some parents didn't value formal education. Often the need to have a child work on the farm, in the shop, or at home took priority over school. Some poor parents couldn't afford to dress their children decently enough to attend school. Students typically had to supply their own books, such as Noah Webster's "blue-backed speller," pictured above, which was actually a reading text.

"I did not go very regularly to school, but by the time I was ten years old I had learned to write, and made a little progress in arithmetic … There was not a grammar, a geography, or a history of any kind in the school. Reading, writing, and arithmetic were the only things taught, and these very indifferently [poorly]."

— Samuel Griswold Goodrich
Recollections of a Lifetime, 1856

HIGHER EDUCATION

Connecticut in the early 1830s offered three options for higher education: Yale University in New Haven; Washington College (now Trinity College) in Hartford; and Wesleyan University in Middletown. None admitted women – nor did any university in the United States, except Oberlin College in Ohio, founded in 1833.

YALE • 1836

Advanced education for women was controversial. Some people claimed studying difficult subjects, like those listed in the Hartford Female Seminary's catalogue shown at right, could damage a woman's "delicate" mind or body. Others believed women were intellectually inferior. Still others feared advanced education would fill young women's heads with learning for which they had no practical use. Such a woman would have a hard time finding a husband, managing a home, and raising a family, which society considered the only proper role for a female.

"[I would] rather my daughters go to school and sit down and do nothing than to study Philosophy, etc. These branches fill young Misses with vanity to the degree that they are above attending to the more useful parts of an education…[turning a girl into] a dandizette at eighteen, and an old maid at thirty."

— Writer in the *Connecticut Courant*, 1830

CHAPTER FOUR
A Golden Opportunity
THE CANTERBURY FEMALE BOARDING SCHOOL, 1831-32

> **BROOKLYN ADVERTISER**
> **November 9, 1831**
>
> *Miss Crandall has lately opened a boarding school exclusively for females, at the village of Canterbury and will teach the following branches, viz, reading, writing, arithmetic, English grammar, geography, ancient and modern together with delineating maps, history, natural and moral philosophy, chemistry and astronomy.*
>
> *There will be no vacation during the year, therefore, scholars can enter or leave at any time without interruption.*
>
> *Books and stationery will be furnished at wholesale price if wanted.*
>
> *The terms of tuition for 12 weeks per term are as follows: "For English studies – $3.00. Board, including washing in the family of the instructress $1.50 per week.*
>
> *Every scholar of the family is required to attend public worship, somewhere, on the Sabbath.*
>
> *In connection with the school. Mr. Andrew Cutler, A.M., will deliver a course of chemical lectures during the coming winter, commencing on Tuesday evening, the 15th day of the present month."*
>
> *The Board of Visitors recommend to the public patronage of Miss Crandall's school and cheerfully add that she has already acquired a high reputation as an instructress and the assiduity and attention which she devotes to the health and morals of her pupils, renders her school a suitable place for education.*

Prudence Crandall had taught in Plainfield for less than a year when seventeen leading citizens of Canterbury proposed that she establish a private school for girls in her hometown. They sweetened the deal by pledging to assist with the cost of setting up the school, send their daughters to it, and help find additional students. It was an offer Prudence couldn't refuse.

The Canterbury citizens who encouraged Prudence to start her school suggested she establish it in the grandest house in town, in the village green neighborhood where many of them lived. The structure, shown at right, built around 1805, boasted 4,000 square feet of space. It was worth 10 times as much as Prudence's father's house.

Prudence bought the house with $500 cash and a $1,500 mortgage. This was another unorthodox step at a time when few women, married or single, owned real estate.

The Canterbury Female Boarding School opened in November of 1831, with Almira Crandall as her sister's assistant. The extensive and demanding curriculum would have done honor to any boys' academy.

American women in the 1830s had few legal rights. Many people were suspicious of, even hostile toward, a female who pursued any calling other than wife and mother, and doubted a woman's ability to perform on the same intellectual level as a man. For the Canterbury Female Boarding School to be socially acceptable and academically credible, it needed the public support and involvement of influential men. A board of visitors that included lawyers, businessmen, and a minister oversaw the school's operation and formally endorsed it.

> **NORWICH COURIER • March 21, 1832**
> *Female Boarding School • Prudence Crandall, Principal*
>
> *The following gentlemen are appointed a Board of Visitors to whom reference may be made for further information.*
>
> *Rufus Adams, Rev. Dennis Platt, Solomon Payne, Andrew Harris, M.D., Deacon William Kinne, Daniel Frost, Daniel Packer, Samuel Hough, Andrew T. Judson*

The Canterbury Female Boarding School's pupils consisted primarily of girls from local families, ranging in age from 8 to 18, who attended during the day. They included Sarah Adams, Eliza and Phoebe Hough, Amy Baldwin, Frances Ensworth, and Mary Clark. Stephen Coit, a Canterbury storekeeper, exchanged supplies for part of the tuition for his daughters Frances and Sarah. He recorded the transaction in his account book, shown at left.

Tuition was $36 for the basic twelve-week term, with additional charges for lessons in drawing, painting, music, or French. Board was an additional $18, and students were responsible for purchasing their own books and supplies. Altogether the cost for twelve weeks at the school for a boarding student amounted to well over $50 – a substantial amount at a time when Prudence could buy the most elegant house in Canterbury for $2,000.

Girls who lived too far from Canterbury to travel back and forth from home to school each day boarded in the school in rooms like the one shown at right. They included Hannah Pearl of Hampton and H.B. Robbins from Lisbon.

TO ALL ON EQUAL TERMS CHAPTER FOUR • OPPORTUNITY

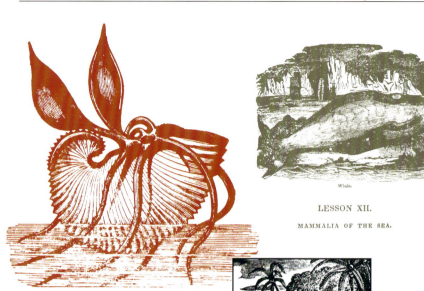

LESSON XXXII.
HABITATIONS—SHELLS—
PEARLS—HABITS—

LESSON XII.
MAMMALIA OF THE SEA.

LESSON XXVIII.

"I hope you have not forgot going down to . . . school to Miss Crandall, and the many pleasant noons we have spent together under the chestnut tree studying our definitions."
— Amy Baldwin to Mary Clark

"*I have met with all the encouragement I ever anticipated.*"
— Prudence Crandall, 1832

Everyone involved with establishing the Canterbury Female Boarding School was thoroughly pleased with the result.

"At a meeting of the Board of Visitors of the Canterbury Female Boarding School on January 20, 1832, Resolved unanimously: That the first quarterly examination of this school has given entire satisfaction to the Board of Visitors."

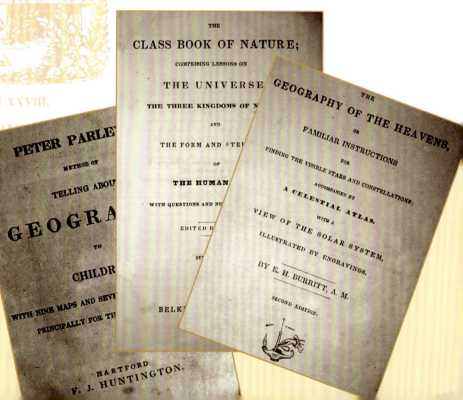

Pupils at the Canterbury Female Boarding School learned from a variety of textbooks that featured what were then state-of-the-art illustrations. *Peter Parley's Method of Telling About Geography to Children*, by children's author Samuel Griswold Goodrich, published in Hartford in 1829, is known to have been one of the works used by Prudence Crandall's students. The young scholars probably studied about astronomy and zoology in books similar to *The Class Book of Nature*, edited by J. Frost, and *The Geography of the Heavens*, by E.H. Burritt, both published in Hartford.

Chapter Five
"To Get a Little More Learning"
A Student of Color Seeks Admission

As the Canterbury Female Boarding School began its second year in the autumn of 1832, Prudence Crandall's circumstances and prospects were bright. She was living in a fine house she herself had bought, in her hometown not far from her family. She was supporting herself doing work she loved, that she considered important, and at which she excelled. She enjoyed the approval and backing of Canterbury's leading citizens. She could look forward to a secure, satisfying career as a respected pioneer of women's education.

But the serenity of Prudence's situation was short-lived. Late in 1832, Sarah Harris, a 20-year-old African-American woman, approached Prudence about attending the all-white Canterbury Female Boarding School.

In her school Prudence employed as a household assistant Mariah Davis, an African-American teenager from Boston. Mariah was engaged to Charles Harris, son of William Harris, an African American who owned a farm in Canterbury, and who was also an agent for *The Liberator*, a radical anti-slavery newspaper published in Boston.

Sarah Harris
Circa 1860s

Mariah Davis loaned copies of *The Liberator* to Prudence. Reading *The Liberator* was an eye-opening experience that would influence Prudence's subsequent actions.

THE LIBERATOR.
IS PUBLISHED WEEKLY
AT NO. 11, MERCHANT'S HALL.
WM. LLOYD GARRISON, EDITOR.

AGENTS.
CONNECTICUT

John Wm. Creed,	New-Haven.
Henry Foster,	Hartford.
Frederick Olney,	Norwich.
William Anderson,	New-London.
William Harris,	Canterbury.

"In that [The Liberator] the condition of the colored people both slaves and free was truthfully portrayed, the double-dealing and manifest deception of the Colonization Society were faithfully exposed, and the question of Immediate Emancipation of the millions of slaves in the United States boldly advocated."
— Prudence Crandall to Ellen Larned, May 15, 1869

Jedidiah Shepard House

When Mariah Davis asked permission to sit in on classes once her chores were completed, Prudence agreed. Mariah's fiancé, Charles Harris, had a twenty-year-old sister, Sarah, who worked as a domestic servant in the house of Jedidiah Shepard in Canterbury. When Sarah visited her future sister-in-law at the Canterbury Female Boarding School, she learned of Mariah's arrangement.

Sarah Harris, described by Prudence as "a colored girl of respectability – a professor of religion – and daughter of honorable parents," was born in 1812 in Norwich, the second eldest of 12 children of William and Sally Harris. Sarah attended a church-sponsored school in Norwich. A family tree sampler, shown at right, attributed to her suggests she received some formal instruction in the feminine art of needlework.

In Norwich, shown in the lithograph below, Sarah was a member of the Second Congregational Church (today the Beulah Land Church of God in Christ), shown at right. In 1832 her father moved his family from Norwich to a farm in Canterbury, where they joined the predominantly white Westminster Congregational Church.

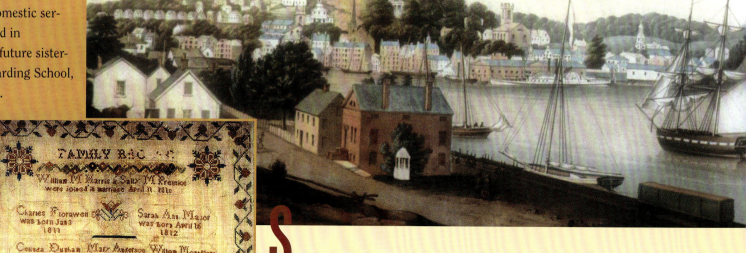

Sarah dreamed of opening her own school for African-American children. To fulfill that ambition she required additional education. Sarah approached Prudence about accepting her as a day student at the Canterbury Female Boarding School.

"Miss Crandall, I want to get a little more learning, if possible, enough to teach colored children, and if you will admit me to your school I shall forever be under the greatest obligation to you."

— Sarah Harris to Prudence Crandall, September, 1832, quoted in *Windham County Advertiser*, May 7, 1833

CHAPTER SIX
No Small Courage
Two Women Stand Up for the Right to an Education

Both Sarah and Prudence expected strong public opposition to a black student at the Canterbury Female Boarding School. To most white people, for an African-American girl to attend a common school was acceptable – for her to receive an elite education alongside the daughters of wealthy white families was intolerable.

Just how intensely most Connecticut residents disapproved of advanced education for African Americans had been demonstrated the previous year. The Reverend Simeon Jocelyn, the white pastor of a black congregation in New Haven, proposed establishing a "college" in that city to provide black men with academic and vocational training. The proposal had aroused a furor in New Haven. Its doom was sealed on September 10, 1831, when a New Haven town meeting voted against it, 700 to 4.

"The location of a college of blacks here [in New Haven] would be totally ruinous to the city . . . whose certain effect will be to lower the town's public morals – to drive from our city its female schools – its throngs of summer visitors – and to stop the vital stream of the city, the influx of young men to Yale College."
— Connecticut Journal, September 9, 1831

Prudence Crandall was an unconventional woman whose liberal opinions on women's education and rights, slavery, and equality of the races most white Americans didn't share. But Prudence wasn't seeking to become a martyr to an unpopular cause. She carefully considered what answer she should give to Sarah Harris. Sarah assured Prudence she would understand if Prudence chose to avoid the trouble admitting Sarah would cause.

"If you think it will be the means of injuring you, I will not insist on the favor."
— Sarah Harris to Prudence Crandall, September, 1832, quoted in *Windham County Advertiser,* May 7, 1833

But Prudence Crandall wasn't one to take the easy way out. Guided by her Quaker upbringing, her religious convictions, and her principles, she made the decision that would alter the course of her life and resonate down through American history.

"Her repeated solicitations were more than my feelings could resist and I told her if I was injured on her account I would bear it – she might enter as one of my pupils."
— Prudence Crandall on Sarah Harris, *Windham County Advertiser*, May 7, 1833

Shortly after Sarah Harris began attending the school, a local minister's wife called on Prudence. She warned that if Sarah Harris were allowed to attend, the parents of white students would withdraw their daughters in protest, forcing the school to close.

"The wife of an Episcopal clergyman who lived in the village told me that if I continued that colored girl in my school, it could not be sustained."
— Prudence Crandall to Ellen Larned, May 15, 1869

Why did Canterbury residents consider one black student attending the Canterbury Female Boarding School so totally unacceptable that they would turn against, even threaten to destroy, the private academy they had actively sought to establish in their town, and with which everyone was thoroughly pleased? To understand the community's extreme reaction, one must look at the history and status of African Americans in Connecticut and the United States, and the moral and political crises over slavery and racial equality that were coming to a head on a national level just as Prudence made her decision to admit Sarah Harris.

Why?

CHAPTER SEVEN

"Truly This Is Our Home"
THE HISTORY OF CONNECTICUT'S BLACK COMMUNITY

The first black people arrived in Connecticut in the mid-1600s, brought as slaves from Africa or the West Indies. By 1774, the eve of the American Revolution, approximately 5,000 African Americans lived in Connecticut, almost all of them slaves. By 1830 there were 8,000 African Americans in the state; by then all but a scattered few were free.

Connecticut in 1830 had the most homogeneous population of any state. The overwhelming majority of its residents were white people of British ancestry. Only three per cent of the state's people were black, and the percentage was just slightly higher in Canterbury. Fifty of Canterbury's 70 black inhabitants lived in the town's 12 African-American households. The remaining 20 resided in white households where they were employed as servants.

SLAVERY

Slaves in Connecticut were legally property. They could be bought, sold, or given away without their consent, as the bill of sale on the right shows. Family members could be separated, never to see each other again.

Slavery didn't take root and flourish in New England as it did below the Mason-Dixon Line. One important reason was that the region's climate and soil weren't suited to raising crops like cotton or tobacco, which required many laborers to cultivate.

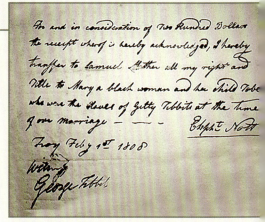

"The trade was made, and we two boys were sold for one hundred pounds a head, lawful money, — yes, sold by a man, a minister of the gospel in Connecticut, the land of steady habits."
— James Mars, *Life of James Mars, a Slave Born and Sold in Connecticut*, 1864

In Connecticut slaves were found in a relatively small number of usually well-to-do households, in ones or twos. In 1790, just 1,563 out of the more than 40,000 households in Connecticut included slaves, with only five owning 10 or more.

Connecticut slaves typically worked as farm laborers and household servants, like the girl watching over a baby in a cradle in the needlework picture at left. Often they lived in the same house as their owners and took their meals with the family.

Connecticut had laws to strictly control the conduct of slaves and free blacks. Slaves couldn't travel outside the town in which they lived without an official pass. They were forbidden to be away from home after 9 p.m. without "special order" from their master or mistress, on penalty of 10 lashes and a fine.

A slave couldn't convey to any free person "goods, money, merchandise, wares, or provisions" without an order from his owner. A slave who threatened to strike a white person could be punished with 30 lashes. Owners could shackle or beat slaves without fear of legal consequences.

"...my master commanded a Negro of his to fetch him a large ox chain. This my master locked on my legs with two padlocks."
— Venture Smith, *A Narrative of the Life and Adventures of Venture, a Native of Africa*, 1798.

Some Connecticut slaves found bondage so intolerable that they tried to escape. Owners sometimes placed advertisements, like this one that a Canterbury resident ran in 1774 in the *Connecticut Courant*, offering a reward for the return of their fugitive property.

EN DOLLARS REWARD.
RUN away from the Subscriber in Canterbury, on the Night following the 26th Instant a ulatto Slave named Sampson, about 5 Feet 8 Inches gh, and thirty Years of Age. He is a Slender ilt Fellow, has thick Lips, a curled, Mulatto Head Hair, uncut, and goes stooping forward. He had and carried with him, when he eloped from his after, a half wore Felt Hat, a black and white wo Shirt, a dark brown Jacket, with Sleeves ffed, and Pewter Buttons down before, a Butter ut coloured Great Coat, with Pewter Buttons, a hite Ditto, a Pair of striped long Trowsers, and a Pair of short hite Ditto, a Pair of white Tow Stockings, and a air of single channel Pumps. Whoever will take said Slave, and deliver him to the Subscriber, in anterbury, shall have the above Reward, and all cessary Charges, paid by me
DANIEL TYLER.
CANTERBURY, June 27, 1774.

A few slaves in Connecticut were permitted to keep any money they could earn in their scarce spare time. Some worked and saved for years until they had enough to buy their own freedom. Venture Smith of Haddam was so proud of this achievement that it was included in his epitaph, shown below. Venture bought the freedom of more than half a dozen other slaves as well.

Sacred to the Memory of Venture Smith, an African, tho the son of a King he was kidnapped & sold as a slave but by his industry he acquired Money to purchase his Freedom who Died Sep 19th 1805 in ye 77th Year of his Age

"Being about forty-six years old, I bought my oldest child, Hannah... I had already redeemed from slavery, myself, my wife and three children, besides three negro men."
— Venture Smith, *A Narrative of the Life and Adventures of Venture, a Native of Africa*, 1798.

During the American Revolution, a number of enslaved men were given, or promised, their freedom on condition that they fight for American independence. To enjoy that liberty, they had to survive the perils of combat and sickness.

Some free blacks took up arms in the cause of American liberty. Lemuel Haynes, born in West Hartford in 1753, served in the Massachusetts militia during the Revolution.

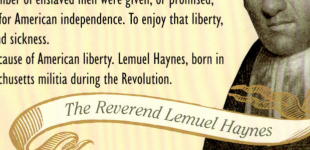
The Reverend Lemuel Haynes

FREEDOM

> **TITLE 96.** *Slavery.*
>
> **An Act to prevent Slavery.**
>
> SECT. 1. BE *it enacted by the Senate and House of Representatives, in General Assembly convened,* That negro and mulatto children, born in this state, shall be free at the age of twenty-one, and shall not be holden in servitude, though their mothers or parents were slaves at their birth.*

Following the Revolution, Connecticut passed legislation to gradually end slavery within its borders. Any child born into bondage in the state after March 1, 1784, would become free at age 25, later reduced to age 21, as shown in the text above.

> SECT. 1. All persons who have been, or shall hereafter, previous to the ratification of this constitution, be admitted freemen, according to the existing laws of this state, shall be electors.
>
> SECT. 2. Every white male citizen of the United States, who shall have gained a settlement in this state, attained the age of twenty-one years; and resided in the town in which he may offer himself to be admitted to the privilege of an elector, at least six months preceding; and have a freehold estate of the yearly value of seven dollars in this state; or having been enrolled in the militia, shall have performed military duty therein, for the term of one year next preceding the time he shall offer himself for admission, or being liable thereto, shall have been, by authority of law, excused therefrom; or shall have paid a state tax within the year next preceding the time he shall present himself for such admission; and shall sustain a good moral character; shall, on his taking such oath as may be prescribed by law, be an elector.
>
> SECT. 3. The privileges of an elector shall be forfeited, by a conviction of bribery, forgery, perjury, duelling,

By 1790, more than half of Connecticut blacks were free. Ten years later fewer than one in five blacks in the state remained in slavery. By 1830, of the approximately 8,000 African Americans living in Connecticut, only 23 were still slaves. But the state didn't officially ban slavery outright until 1848. Nancy Toney of Windsor, the last surviving person to have been a slave in Connecticut, died in 1857.

Slavery was almost totally eradicated from Connecticut during the 50 years prior to Prudence Crandall opening her school. But the change had occurred so quickly and recently that any adult past age 50 could personally remember a time when half the state's blacks were still slaves. A great many free blacks living in Connecticut were former slaves. And slavery still flourished in the South, where millions of black men, women, and children were held in bondage. These realities, and the prejudices that accompanied them, shaped the attitudes and actions of blacks and whites alike.

Nancy Toney

James Mars

"I was told when a slave boy, that some of the people said that slaves had no souls, and that they would never go to heaven, let them do ever so well."
— James Mars, *Life of James Mars, a Slave Born and Sold in Connecticut,* 1864

Freedom didn't mean equality for Connecticut African Americans. Although more than 400 Connecticut black men had enlisted in the war for American independence, and all blacks were required to pay taxes the same as whites, the Connecticut state constitution of 1818, shown at left, denied African Americans the right to vote.

Prejudice against blacks was widespread and publicly expressed in Connecticut in the 1830s.

"[Some black residents of Hartford] told me it was hardly safe for them to be in the streets alone at night. To pelt them with stones ... as they pass seems to be the pastime of the place."
— Edward Strutt Abdy, *Journal of a Residence and Tour in the United States of North America,* 1835

One of slavery's crippling legacies was the fact that most blacks lacked the training or education to follow a trade, or money to purchase farm land, and had little hope of acquiring any. This meant most could find only low-paying, unskilled manual labor jobs like those held by many African Americans listed in the Hartford City Directory for 1848, shown below.

"[Blacks in Connecticut are] excluded, directly or virtually, from many employments, (for the whites will not work with them) and…despised in all…"
— Edward Strutt Abdy, *Journal of a Residence and Tour in the United States of North America*, 1835

Colored Persons.

Adams Henry, laborer, h Cooper Lane
Adams Lewis, barber, b Cooper Lane
Adams John, laborer, h Cooper Lane
Adams Walter, h Cooper Lane
Africanus Selah, teacher, h 37 Village
Austin William, waiter at American Hotel
Augustus Ezekiel, laborer, h 40 Elm
Asher Edwin, laborer, h Cooper Lane
Babcock Susan, washwoman, h Wethersfield lane
Babcock Thomas, cook, b Bliss st
Brewster Maria widow, h 54 Front
Bowers Ann, washwoman, h Wethersfield Lane
Brown Alanson, porter, 85 State
Burkhardt Miss Louisa, dress maker, b Franklin st
Brooks Herod, b 26 Main
Brown Robert, waiter, h rear 2 Ann
Brown Benjamin, laborer, h near north burying ground
Baxter Sarah, h 8 Talcott
Cambridge Ichabod, laborer, h near N. Bur'g Ground
Camp George, laborer, h near north burying ground
Camp Shem, laborer, h near north burying ground
Camp Philip, laborer, h near north burying ground
Camp Philip jr. laborer, h near north burying ground
Carrier Hezekiah, seaman, h Charles st
Carter James, cook at Clinton House, b 40 Elm
Carey Lot, cook at City Hotel
Clark Mary widow, h 40 Elm
Cross Amos, h north end Front
Cross Isaac, h rear 2 Ann
Champion Henry, coachman, h Coles st
Champion Edward A. laborer, h Coles st

Most rural blacks farmed a small piece of land and also did manual labor for whites. A few picked up a trade, such as chimney sweep, cooper, comb maker, shoemaker, or blacksmith. Some black men found employment as sailors aboard ships that went out from ports in Connecticut and Rhode Island.

Black women frequently worked as domestics in the houses of well-to-do whites. Canterbury residents who employed African-American servants included Daniel Packer, Stephen Coit, Richard Fenner, and Chauncey Bacon.

Occasionally an African-American individual managed to acquire the training and resources to establish himself as an independent farmer or businessman. One such success story was Isaac Glasko, who started a blacksmithing shop in Griswold, Connecticut, in 1806. Glasko's shop expanded into a forge employing 10 men, known for the quality of the tools it produced, including harpoons, lances, and spades. The section of Griswold in which his forge was located became known officially as Glasko, shown on the 1868 map at right.

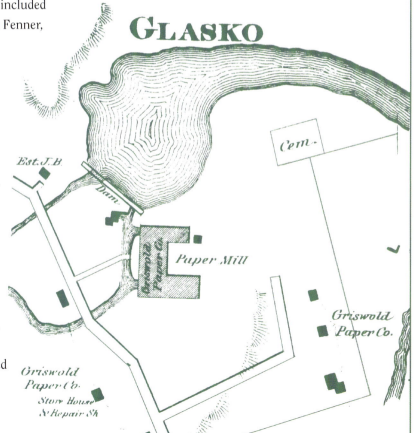

EDUCATION

African-American children sometimes attended common schools. But cruel prejudice and bigotry could make seeking an education a nightmarish experience. Black students sometimes managed to obtain a decent education even under these separate, unequal conditions. The first teacher at Colchester's segregated common school was a remarkable young black man named Prince Saunders, who went on to become an anti-slavery activist and a leader in the development of an educational system for newly liberated slaves in Haiti.

Some black parents, convinced their children could never get a decent education in the hostile atmosphere of an integrated common school, asked their towns to establish separate common schools for black children alone. At the request of the African-American community, a separate common school for black students was established in Hartford. The Reverend James Pennington, pastor of the Talcott Street Congregational Church, was head teacher in the 1840s.

Some towns formally segregated their common schools. In 1803 Colchester used an unexpected bequest to build a splendid new three-story school, the Bacon Academy, shown to the left of the Congregational church on the town green in the engraving above. But the town's African-American children weren't welcome at the Bacon Academy. Instead, beginning in 1806, they were taught by black teachers paid by the town in the abandoned common school building, hidden in the trees to the right of the meetinghouse in the above engraving.

Reverend James Pennington

SCHOOLS.—FIRE DEPARTMENT.   121
COLORED DISTRICT SCHOOL, 12 Talcott street.
Rev. J. C. Pennington, *Teacher.*
Mrs. Pennington, *Assistant.*

In Memory of
Boston Trow trow
Govener of ye Affri
Can Trib he Died
May 28th 1772
Aet 66

COMMUNITY

Few in number and scattered as they were, Connecticut's African Americans nonetheless sought to connect as a community. From the mid-1700s into the early 1800s in several communities, the black residents, both slave and free, annually elected a "black governor." Although this man had no authority under the law, he was respected by the African-American population, over whom he exercised considerable influence. Boston Trow Trow, a slave of Jedidiah Huntington, was black governor of Norwich from 1770 to 1772, a distinction noted on his gravestone in the Old Norwichtown Cemetery.

Once free, many blacks from around the state gravitated toward cities. There the opportunities for work were greater and strength of numbers improved their chances of bettering their situation and finding a spouse.

If securing the basics of an education was difficult for an African American in Connecticut, higher education was almost an impossibility. In 1833 Amos Beman, son of the Reverend Jehiel Beman, pastor of Middletown's African Methodist Episcopal Zion Church, was denied admission to Wesleyan University, shown at left, in that city. Undaunted, Amos Beman arranged for a sympathetic white Wesleyan student to tutor him privately.

Beman studied for about six months, until a dozen Wesleyan students sent him an anonymous note, threatening him with physical harm if he didn't cease his studies. Amos Beman left Wesleyan, which the following year adopted a policy of accepting black students.

"Young Beman: — a number of the students of this University deeming it derogatory to themselves, as well as to the University, to have you and other colored students recite here, do hereby warn you to desist from such a course; and if you fail to comply with this peaceable request, we swear, by the Eternal God, that we will resort to forcible means to put a stop to it.

Twelve of Us"

— Anonymous Wesleyan University students to Amos Beman, October 5, 1833

The church became central to urban black community life during the first half of the 1800s. African Americans fed-up with second-class treatment in white churches, which included being segregated in the least desirable seats, formed their own congregations, usually led by black ministers. In 1819 African-American members of Hartford's First Congregational Church began holding their own separate services. In 1826 they established the Talcott Street Congregational Church, and built their own house of worship, shown at left. Black churches were established around the same time in Middletown, Norwich, and Stonington. In 1847, the New Haven City Directory, shown at right, listed black churches of several denominations.

```
FIRST BAPTIST CHURCH.
    Chapel Street, near Olive.
Rev. S. Dryden Phelps, Pastor.  Nathan Thomas, Eliphalet Cooper,
Wm. Forbes, Wm. S. Harrimount, Deacons.  Samuel A. Van, Clerk.
Geo. B. Rich, Treasurer.

SECOND BAPTIST CHURCH.
    Academy, Corner of Greene Street.
Rev. O. B. Judd, Pastor.  Henry Alling, Lyman Miller, Miner K.
Frisbie, Deacons.  Jos. Angell, Clerk.  Abijah Hoyt, Treasurer.

CHRIST'S CHURCH, (ROMAN CATHOLIC.)
    Corner of Davenport Avenue and York Streets.
Rev. James Smyth, Priest.

WESLEYAN M. E. ZION CHURCH, (COLORED.)
    Broad Street.
Rev. Mr. Simmons, Pastor.  Stephen Ajom, Henry Berrien, Robert
Fuller, Francis Cisco, Christian Heitman, Thomas Jones, Trustees.

BETHEL CHURCH, (COLORED.)
    Whalley Avenue.

TEMPLE ST. CONGREGATIONAL CHURCH, (COLORED.)
    Temple Street.
Rev. Amos G. Beman, Pastor.  A. C. Luca, Luke Lathrop, Deacons.

ST. LUKE'S (EPISCOPAL) CHURCH, (COLORED.)
    Gregson Street.
Rev. E. W. Stokes, Pastor.

THIRD BAPTIST CHURCH, (COLORED.)
    York Street.
Rev. Samuel B. Serrington, Pastor.
```

CHAPTER EIGHT
The Voice of Conscience Grows Louder
SEARCHING FOR SOLUTIONS TO SLAVERY AND RACISM

The issues of slavery and the role of free blacks in American society were just beginning to be addressed on the national level at the time Prudence Crandall made her fateful decision. Although slavery was virtually extinct in Connecticut, a growing number of people in the state, along with others in New England and across the North, were increasingly disturbed by the fact that it continued to thrive elsewhere in the United States, as shown in the broadside at left.

In the South, blacks in bondage were often poorly fed, clothed, and housed, and worked ruthlessly. Slaves were kept under control by a harsh system of laws and customs that prohibited them from traveling without permission, learning to read, or taking any recourse against a white individual who harmed them in any way. Slaves were bought and sold like livestock; families were frequently torn apart, never to see each other again. Owners could physically abuse and exploit slaves with unimaginable brutality and even kill them, without fear of legal punishment.

Many individuals were also disturbed by discrimination against free blacks throughout the country. Men and women, black and white, began seeking a solution.

COLONIZATION

By 1817, the American Colonization Society had been formed, "for the laudable purpose of extirpating from the nation the deep and deadly disgrace of slavery." Their solution was to settle free people of color and emancipated slaves in a new colony on the northwestern coast of Africa, shown on the map at right, optimistically given the noble name of "Liberia." No black person would be forced to leave America for Africa. Any who went to Liberia would do so voluntarily.

> "Anything like a social or domestic equality between the two races can never be enjoyed."
> — Wilbur Fisk, *Substance of an Address Delivered Before the Middletown Colonization Society*, 1835

Wilbur Fisk

Colonizationists were motivated not only by a desire to eliminate slavery from America, but also by the conviction that blacks and whites could never live together in harmony. Some colonizationists believed blacks were "innately degraded," claiming they were "destitute of means, motives, and energy of character." Others felt that the destructive effects of slavery and white racism would make it impossible for blacks ever to prosper in the United States.

> **NOTICE.**
> On Tuesday evening next, 6 o'clock, at the State-House, there will be a meeting of our citizens, both of this and other towns, who may please to attend, for a choice of officers of the Auxiliary Colonization Society for the benefit of the people of color. Hartford, Oct. 14.

Colonizationists contended they had the welfare of blacks in mind. The list of officers of the Hartford Auxiliary of the Colonization Society elected in a meeting at the Old State House in 1819 read like a "who's who" of influential and powerful state leaders.

> "The colonization scheme will have a powerful tendency to produce the gradual emancipation of those now in **bondage** in this land of **freedom**. It is a fact that a strong desire exists in the breasts of many slave holders, in the Southern Atlantic states, to emancipate."
> — John S. Peters, *Constitution of the Hartford Auxiliary Colonization Society*, 1819

One of colonizationists' greatest fears was "the conjugal union, and the domestic amalgamation of the two colors" – interracial marriage. Terror of amalgamation had already shut down the Foreign Mission School founded in Cornwall, Connecticut, in 1817 to educate Asians, Hawaiians, Africans, Native Americans, and other "infidels" to become Christian missionaries among their own people. In 1826, when two young women from prominent local families married Cherokee Indians who were students at the school, Cornwall was scandalized. Harriet Gold, engaged to Cherokee Indian Elias Boudinot, was burned in effigy by enraged townspeople. Elias and Harriet married nonetheless, and went to live on the Cherokee reservation in Georgia. The Cornwall Mission School closed in 1827.

African Americans indignantly rejected colonization. In July of 1831 black residents of Middletown met at the African Methodist Episcopal Zion Church (of which the Reverend Jehiel Beman, the son of a former slave who had fought in the American Revolution, was pastor) to declare their intention to remain in the land of their birth. Colonization was a complete failure. During the American Colonization Society's more than 40 years of operation, only about 12,000 blacks moved to Liberia. Between 1830 and 1850, a mere ten blacks emigrated from Connecticut.

> "Why should we leave this land so dearly bought by the blood, groans and tears of our fathers? Truly this is our home: here let us live, and here let us die."
> — Resolution of a meeting of the Colored Citizens of Middletown, Connecticut, July 18, 1831

ABOLITION

In the North, concern was growing about the injustice and hypocrisy of allowing slavery to exist anywhere in the United States. Many who initially embraced colonization as a solution to this great national sin came to see it as both unworkable and unjust to African Americans. By the early 1830s a small but growing number of people, including many one-time colonizationists, became convinced that the answer was to abolish slavery throughout America.

The most radical abolitionists demanded immediate, total, unconditional emancipation, and full equality for blacks. One colonizationist-turned-abolitionist was William Lloyd Garrison of Boston, editor of *The Liberator*, for which the masthead is shown above. *The Liberator* had opened Prudence Crandall's eyes to so much that was wrong about slavery, colonization, and the treatment of free blacks. Garrison made clear, in the statement shown at left, his uncompromising dedication to the abolitionist cause.

> I am aware, that many object to the severity of my language; but is there not cause for severity? I *will be* as harsh as truth, and as uncompromising as justice. On this subject, I do not wish to think, or speak, or write, with moderation. No! no! Tell a man whose house is on fire, to give a moderate alarm; tell him to moderately rescue his wife from the hands of the ravisher; tell the mother to gradually extricate her babe from the fire into which it has fallen;—but urge me not to use moderation in a cause like the present. I am in earnest—I will not equivocate—I will not excuse—I will not retreat a single inch—AND I WILL BE HEARD. The apathy of the people is enough to make every statue leap from its pedestal, and to hasten the resurrection of the dead.

Abolitionism was slowly gaining adherents in Connecticut in the early 1830s. But most Americans, New Englanders included, opposed the abolitionist movement. They feared abolitionists would stir up slave rebellions in the South, that their activities would anger citizens of the slave states, alienate them from the North, and perhaps even result in the breaking up of the Union. An anti-abolitionist statement, shown at right, was published in Hartford in 1835. It urged citizens to condemn and put a stop to abolitionists' "violent measures."

A DECLARATION
OF THE SENTIMENTS OF THE PEOPLE OF HARTFORD, REGARDING THE MEASURES OF THE

Abolitionists.

CONSIDERING that it is no less the *duty* than the right of freemen, to express their sentiments on all questions materially affecting the prosperity of the country or the maintenance of its liberties and free institutions; and regarding the moral force of public opinion as the basis and primary elemental principle of our government, *the Citizens of Hartford* cannot view with indifference the excitement which now prevails on the subject of slavery in the United States.

This excitement has been occasioned by the rash and reckless measures and proceedings of the Abolitionists of the Middle and Northern States. We believe that these proceedings will result in no good, but much evil; that their direct and obvious tendency is to agitate and alarm the people of the slave States; endanger their peace and security, if not expose them to the evils and horrors of insurrection, massacre and a servile war—to injure the slave population and subject them to restrictions and severities from which they have hitherto been exempt, and greatly defer, if not wholly extinguish the hope of the final amelioration of their condition—that they tend to destroy that reciprocal harmony and confidence which should prevail among the people of different sections of the Union; to embarrass commercial and social intercourse among them, to alienate their minds and to "weaken those sacred ties which hold together its several parts."

And furthermore, we believe, and declare, that the conduct of the Abolitionists, in distributing their incendiary publications—not discussing the subject of slavery, but addressed only to the passions of a degraded and servile population—in the slave holding States, in violation of their laws and in contravention of the spirit of the constitution of the United States, which guarantees to each State the exclusive regulation of all local interests, including that of master and slave, is wholly unjustifiable—a contempt of public opinion, a flagrant outrage against the society which affords them protection, and a high *offence* against the *principles of morality*, because their whole conduct is predicated on a total recklessness of consequences, which can only proceed from depravity of heart or desperate infatuation.

With these views of the subject, we declare our solemn conviction, that it is the duty of all good citizens, by word,

Chapter Nine
Seizing the Sword of Truth
Prudence Crandall Confounds Her Critics

The atmosphere in Connecticut was explosive as Prudence Crandall struggled to decide whether to dismiss Sarah Harris from her school. Within the span of two generations the state's population, culture, economy, and government had experienced profound changes, including the liberation of thousands of African-American slaves.

Free blacks in Connecticut were coming together in communities, establishing churches, schools, and other organizations to improve their current circumstances and create opportunities for a better future. They were publicly discussing, even demanding, equal rights and opportunities. The increasing boldness and potential for power of people who not so long ago had been legally property was threatening to many whites in Connecticut and aggravated the racism that had always existed.

Tensions were rising across the country as a growing number of abolitionists made increasingly radical demands, while those who feared anti-slavery agitation would destroy the nation sought to silence them by any means possible. The issues of slavery and African-American rights were flaring into a national crisis. Any action, no matter how small, that seemed likely to fan the flames was cause for alarm.

In considering her response to the ultimatum that Sarah Harris be barred from her school, Prudence looked to the Bible for guidance. One particular passage from the Book of Ecclesiastes, shown below, impressed her.

> SO I returned, and considered all the oppressions that are done under the sun; and behold the tears of such as were oppressed, and they *had* no comforter: and on the side of their oppressors *there was* power, but they *had* no comforter.
>
> *Ecclesiastes 4:1*

"I said in my heart, here are my convictions. What shall I do? Shall I be inactive and permit prejudice, 'The mother of abominations' to remain undisturbed? Or shall I venture to enlist in the ranks of those who with the Sword of Truth dare hold combat with prevailing iniquity? I contemplated for a while the manner in which I might best serve the people of color. As wealth was not mine, I saw no other means of benefitting [sic] them, than by imparting to those of my own sex that were anxious to learn, all the instruction I might be able to give, however small the amount."

— Prudence Crandall, *Windham County Herald*, May 7, 1833

> "The wife of an Episcopal clergyman who lived in the village told me that if I continued that colored girl in my school, it could not be sustained."
> — Prudence Crandall to Ellen Larned, May 15, 1869

Prudence Crandall refused to be intimidated by the minister's wife's warning that the Canterbury Female Boarding School would go under if a black student were allowed to attend.

"I replied to her, That it might sink, then, for I should not turn her out!"
— Prudence Crandall to Ellen Larned, May 15, 1869, quoted in *History of Windham County, Volume II*, 1880

Prudence then took an even more controversial step that soon put Canterbury in the national spotlight.

"I made up my mind that if it were possible I would teach colored girls exclusively."
— Prudence Crandall to Ellen Larned, May 15, 1869, quoted in *History of Windham County, Volume II*, 1880

Arthur Tappan

William Lloyd Garrison

Prudence met in Boston with William Lloyd Garrison. Garrison and other abolitionists realized that enrolling African-American students from outside Connecticut in Prudence's new academy would force a public debate on whether blacks were citizens entitled to full rights under the U.S. Constitution, including the right to attend school in any state. Garrison pledged his support to Prudence, and gave her the names of African-American families in several Northeastern cities who might be interested in sending their daughters to her school. She followed up his leads with visits to Providence and New York to recruit students for her new all-black academy.

During her recruiting trips Prudence gained the support of the Reverend Simeon Jocelyn of New Haven; abolitionist George Benson, Jr., of Providence, and his brother, Henry, an agent for *The Liberator*; Arnold Buffum, president of the New England Antislavery Society; and wealthy New York City merchant and abolitionist Arthur Tappan. All were outspoken advocates of immediate emancipation of slaves. Essential and welcome as their backing was, it also inevitably connected Prudence in the public mind to the highly controversial abolitionist movement.

Chapter Ten
Raging Bullies
The Battle of Canterbury Begins

On February 24, 1833, Prudence Crandall told her white students that when the school's next term began on April 1 it would accept only black girls. The following morning four of Canterbury's leading citizens – attorney Daniel Frost, Jr., Dr. Andrew Harris, justice of the peace Rufus Adams, and merchant Richard Fenner – appeared at Prudence's house to warn her against going through with her plan.

Prudence expected her proposal to upset many people, but she wasn't prepared for the rage from residents of Canterbury and surrounding communities. There was great concern that such a school would prove false the widely held belief that blacks were intellectually inferior, and raise the disturbing idea of equality between the races. The school's location on the green, in the finest house in town, made Prudence's idea particularly distressing to her prestigious neighbors. Her former backers may have felt betrayed by this woman whom they had welcomed and supported.

On March 1, Prudence was again visited by a delegation of leading citizens who objected to her proposed school.

"[Dr. Andrew Harris warned that if Prudence Crandall] received her expected scholars, the blacks of the town … would begin to look up and claim an equality with the whites; and if they were all placed upon an equal footing property and life would no longer be safe."
— George Benson to William Lloyd Garrison, March 5, 1833

At the end of February, William Lloyd Garrison wrote about Prudence's plight to the Reverend Samuel J. May, shown at right, the young activist pastor of the Unitarian Church in Brooklyn, Connecticut, not far from Canterbury. May immediately sent Prudence a letter assuring her of his wholehearted support.

"I determined to do all in my power to assist you."
— Samuel May to Prudence Crandall, February 27, 1833

Prudence announced her plan to the world in an ad in *The Liberator* on March 2, 1833. A board of prominent male supporters was as essential to the success of Prudence's academy for African-American girls as it had been to her school for white students. James Forten, a wealthy sailmaker and anti-slavery activist in Philadelphia, was one of the prominent African-American leaders on her new board, which also included the Reverend Jehiel Beman of the African Methodist Episcopal Zion Church in Middletown; the Reverend Peter Williams of St. Philip's African Church in New York City; and the Reverend Samuel C. Cornish, co-founder in New York of *Freedom's Journal*, the first black-owned and operated newspaper in America.

James Forten

PRUDENCE CRANDALL,
PRINCIPAL OF THE CANTERBURY, (CONN.) FEMALE
BOARDING SCHOOL.

RETURNS her most sincere thanks to those who have patronized her School, and would give information that on the first Monday of April next, her School will be opened for the reception of young Ladies and little Misses of color. The branches taught are as follows:— Reading, Writing, Arithmetic, English Grammar, Geography, History, Natural and Moral Philosophy, Chemistry, Astronomy, Drawing and Painting, Music on the Piano, together with the French language.

☞ The terms, including board, washing, and tuition, are $25 per quarter, one half paid in advance.

☞ Books and Stationary will be furnished on the most reasonable terms.

For information respecting the School, reference may be made to the following gentlemen, viz.—

ARTHUR TAPPAN, Esq.
Rev. PETER WILLIAMS,
Rev. THEODORE RAYMOND,
Rev. THEODORE WRIGHT,   } N. YORK CITY.
Rev. SAMUEL C. CORNISH,
Rev. GEORGE BOURNE,
Rev. Mr. HAYBORN,
Mr. JAMES FORTEN,   } PHILADELPHIA.
Mr. JOSEPH CASSEY,
Rev. S. J. MAY,—BROOKLYN, CT.
Rev. Mr. BEMAN,—MIDDLETOWN, CT.
Rev. S. S. JOCELYN,—NEW-HAVEN, CT.
Wm. LLOYD GARRISON,   } BOSTON, MASS.
ARNOLD BUFFUM,
GEORGE BENSON,—PROVIDENCE, R.I.

A special town meeting was called in Canterbury on March 9 to address the crisis. Since it would be considered socially inappropriate for a woman to attend and address a town meeting, Prudence authorized Samuel May and Arnold Buffum to speak for her. The Canterbury meetinghouse, which reportedly could hold a thousand people, was packed for the meeting.

At the meeting, influential attorney Andrew Judson, Prudence's next-door neighbor and a member of the Board of Visitors for the original Canterbury Female Boarding School, launched a vicious attack on the proposed academy for black girls. Judson, who considered the Canterbury controversy an opportunity to advance his political ambitions, which included a possible run for governor, would become Prudence's chief nemesis.

> "*He [Judson] twanged every chord that could stir the coarser passions of the human heart and with such success that his hearers seemed to be filled with the apprehension that a dire calamity was impending over them, and that Miss C. was the author or instrument of it …*"
>
> — Rev. Samuel May to *The Liberator*, March, 1833

Attorney Andrew T. Judson

When Samuel. May and Arnold Buffum tried to speak in Prudence's defense, they were bullied into silence.

> "*Gentlemen sprang to their feet in hot displeasure; and with fists doubled in our faces roughly admonished us that if we opened our lips there, they would inflict upon us the utmost penalty of the law if not a more immediate vengeance.*"
>
> — Rev. Samuel May to *The Liberator*, March, 1833

The idea of an elite school for African-American girls elicited a contemptuous comment from Catharine Beecher, founder of the renowned Hartford Female Seminary.

> "**There are not a dozen coloured families in New England, in such pecuniary circumstances, that if they were white it would not be thought ridiculous to attempt to give their daughters such a course of education.**"
>
> — Catharine Beecher, *An Essay on Slavery and Abolitionism*, 1837

Catharine Beecher

Andrew Judson's fear-mongering went unchallenged and infected the town meeting almost to a man.

> *"The obvious tendency of a school for black girls would be to collect within the town of Canterbury large numbers of persons from other States whose characters and habits might be various and unknown to us, thereby rendering insecure the persons, property and reputations of our citizens."*
>
> — Canterbury Town Meeting resolution, March 9, 1833

But Buffum and May were determined Prudence's side should be heard. Once the formal town meeting was adjourned, Rev. May called for the attention of the crowd; about half stayed to hear him. When the church trustees shut the meetinghouse doors, May and Buffum continued their defense of Prudence on the town green. Rev. May stated that admitting black students to a private academy in a small rural Connecticut town was an issue of interest to people far beyond Canterbury or Connecticut.

> *"The question between us is not simply whether thirty or forty colored girls shall be well educated at a school to be kept in Canterbury; but whether the people in any part of the land will recognize and generously protect the 'inalienable rights of man' without distinction of color."*
>
> — Rev. Samuel May, March 9, 1833

A few days after the town meeting, Andrew Judson came to Rev. Samuel May's house in Brooklyn, shown at right, to clarify his behavior. The minister's unwavering support of Prudence infuriated Judson.

> *"The colored people can never rise from their menial condition in our country; they ought not to be permitted to rise here. They are an inferior race of beings, and never can or ought to be recognized as the equals of whites ... The condition of the colored population can never be essentially improved on this continent."*
>
> — Andrew Judson to Rev. Samuel May, March, 1833

Garrison reported on the Canterbury controversy in *The Liberator*, heaping scorn upon Prudence's opponents. Prudence and her supporters urged him to tone down the rhetoric, so as not to "heighten the flame of malignity among" the residents of Canterbury. But Garrison was incapable of restraint when addressing slavery or racism. Local newspapers ran articles and letters about the Canterbury Female Boarding School, which was soon debated in the press far beyond Connecticut.

As soon as Prudence started her school for "young Ladies and little Misses of color" on April 1, her opponents intensified their campaign of intimidation. A gathering of Canterbury residents on April 5 resolved to boycott Prudence, refusing to sell her supplies or provide services. The lone dissenter was storekeeper Stephen Coit, whose daughters had attended Prudence's all-white academy. Although Coit was "violently opposed" to Prudence's school for African-American students, he continued to do business with Prudence. Another Canterbury merchant, Edward Jenks, also dared to sell supplies to Prudence as the page from his account book, shown at left, records. Despite the ugly furor, a determined Prudence moved forward with her school.

"Miss Crandall ... is as undaunted as if she had a whole world on her side. She has opened her school and is resolved to persevere." — William Lloyd Garrison to Isaac Knapp, April 11, 1833

CHAPTER ELEVEN

Adding Prosecution to Persecution
Using Old and New Laws to Close the Canterbury Female Boarding School

When it became clear that intimidation wouldn't stop Prudence Crandall, Canterbury residents turned to the law. On April 1, a Canterbury town meeting voted to petition the Connecticut General Assembly for "some law by which the introduction of foreign [out-of-state] blacks, might be regulated in a proper degree by the feelings and wishes of the inhabitants of the towns."

In the meantime, Canterbury leaders sought to use existing laws, like the one shown below, to rid themselves of the black students.

In Connecticut each town was legally responsible for supporting its poor residents. Newcomers who hadn't been accepted as residents, and who seemed likely to need financial assistance, could be "warned out" – ordered to leave town subject to harsh penalties.

On April 13, 1833, Sheriff Roger Coit appeared at the Canterbury Female Boarding School with a writ warning out Ann Eliza Hammond, 17, a black student who had arrived from Providence the previous day. Rev. Samuel May's offer to post bond to guarantee Ann Eliza wouldn't become a financial burden on Canterbury was turned down. Her enemies' latest tactic failed to change Prudence's determination.

On April 22, ten days after Ann Eliza Hammond had arrived in Canterbury, Sheriff Coit returned with a summons for her to appear before a justice of the peace on May 2. The charge was failure to leave Canterbury as ordered and failure to pay the $1.67 fine for remaining in town without permission. When a $1,000 bond was offered as security for any damage Ann Eliza Hammond or any other students of the Canterbury Female Boarding School might cause, the selectmen accepted.

The legal harassment of Ann Eliza Hammond was covered in the newspapers well beyond the Northeast. A broadside, shown below, printed to spread word of the oppression, called application of the law against Ann Eliza Hammond "A Doctrine so monstrous, that none but Fools and Knaves would attempt to enforce it."

SECT. 7. The select-men of any town shall be, and they are hereby authorized, either by themselves, or by warrant from a justice of the peace, in such town, directed to either constable of such town, which warrant such justice is hereby authorized to give, to warn any person not an inhabitant of this state, to depart such town; and the person so warned, shall forfeit and pay to the treasurer of such town, one dollar and sixty-seven cents per week, for every week he or she shall continue in such town, after warning given as aforesaid, (and when any such person, who shall be convicted of the breach of this act, in refusing to depart on warning as aforesaid, hath no estate to satisfy the fine, such person shall be whipped on the naked body, not exceeding ten stripes, unless he or she depart the town within ten days next after sentence given, and reside no more therein)* without leave of the select-men. Provided nevertheless, that nothing contained in this section, or

"*I* have put my hand to the plough and I will never no never look back ... in the midst of this affliction I am as happy as at any moment of my life ..."
— Prudence Crandall to Simeon Jocelyn, April 17, 1833

BARBARISM.

Who are now the savages? The Indians, the Georgians, or the Persecutors of the noble minded Miss Prudence Crandall, of Canterbury, and her excellent pupil Miss Eliza Ann Hammond of Providence? Will Andrew T. Judson, for himself and his Canterbury associates, answer the interrogation? – Community and posterity will answer it for them.

Do they suppose that the letter of the law which they plead as authority for barbarism, would be the rule of judgment with men of sense, to exclude persons from other States in the Union, of good character, from the priviliges of education in this State, and who are able to pay for those privileges? If so, the Civil Authority of Hartford may warn every Student from other States out of the City – fine them—and on refusing to pay the fine or to leave the place, give each at the whipping post ten lashes upon the naked body, and remove them to whence they came. The President of each of our Colleges, and the Principals of every Boarding School in the State, can be fined for educating such persons - *a Doctrine so monstrous, that none but Fools and Knaves would attempt to enforce it.*

THE IMPERIAL ORDER of the Persecutors of Miss Eliza Ann Hammond

"*S*hame to the Persecutors! Burning shame to the gallant and noble Inflictors of Stripes upon innocent and studious Females!!!" — *Barbarism*, broadside, 1833

For some of Prudence's black students, the Canterbury Female Boarding School was a unique opportunity for an education. Ann Eliza Hammond and her sister Sarah Lloyd Hammond were the daughters of a widowed boardinghouse keeper in Providence. Harriet Rosette Lanson of New Haven was the daughter of impoverished alcoholics, who had been removed as a child from "an abode of wretchedness and vice," and made the ward of the Reverend Simeon Jocelyn. Jocelyn, who was not a wealthy man, arranged for Harriet to attend the Canterbury school in exchange for helping with housework.

But several African-American pupils at the Canterbury Female Boarding School could have acquired just as good an education in their hometowns. Elizabeth Douglass Bustill came from one of the oldest, most respected African-American families in Philadelphia, where there were several good schools for black students. One school to which many of the city's most prominent African-American families sent their children was operated by Elizabeth's cousin, Sarah Mapps Douglass. Theodosia Degrass, Ann Peterson, Ann Elizabeth Wiles, M.E. Carter, G.C. Marshal, and Catherine Ann Weldon came from New York City, which boasted the excellent African Free School, supported by the city. That these girls' parents sent them to school in Canterbury, a hotbed of controversy that would likely grow worse, was a demonstration of their support for African Americans' rights to equal education and all other benefits of citizenship.

Even as the situation grew increasingly tense, new students arrived at the Canterbury Female Boarding School. By early May Prudence had more than 17 pupils; ultimately more than two dozen would attend.

Some of Prudence's African-American students came from Connecticut. Most were from Philadelphia, New York City, Providence, and Boston.

Providence, RI to Canterbury, CT	30 miles
New York City to Canterbury, CT	115 miles
Philadelphia, PA to Canterbury, CT	215 miles
Boston, MA to Canterbury, CT	75 miles

The new students settled into a normal school routine. They pursued their studies despite occasional reminders, like cow manure and eggs thrown against the house, that they weren't welcome in Canterbury.

"Love and union seem to bind our little circle in the bonds of sisterly affection."
— Anonymous African-American student at Canterbury Female Boarding School to *The Liberator*, July 6, 1833

"… the colored scholars under my care made as good, if not better progress than the same number of whites taken from the same positions in life."
— Prudence Crandall to Ellen Larned, July 2, 1869

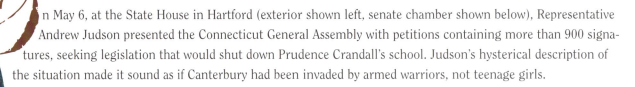

On May 6, at the State House in Hartford (exterior shown left, senate chamber shown below), Representative Andrew Judson presented the Connecticut General Assembly with petitions containing more than 900 signatures, seeking legislation that would shut down Prudence Crandall's school. Judson's hysterical description of the situation made it sound as if Canterbury had been invaded by armed warriors, not teenage girls.

"The establishment or rendezvous falsely denominated a school was designed by its projectors as the theatre, as the place to promulgate their disgusting doctrines of amalgamation and their pernicious sentiments of subverting the union. These pupils are to be congregated here from all quarters under the pretense of educating them but really to scatter fire brands, arrows and death among brethren of our own blood."
— Andrew Judson to Connecticut General Assembly, April, 1833

The General Assembly also heard from Pardon Crandall, who sent a letter boldly encouraging them to defeat the proposed legislation.

"I entreat the members of the Assembly when acting on this petition to remember those self evident truths that all mankind are created free and equal, that they are endowed with inalienable rights of which no man nor any set of men have any right to deprive them. And my request is that you will not ... pass any act which will curtail or destroy any of the rights of free people of this state or other states whether they are white or black."
— Pardon Crandall to the Connecticut General Assembly, May 1, 1833

A committee, chaired by State Senator Phillip Pearl of Hampton, whose daughter had attended Prudence's all-white school, endorsed the legislation.

"Although the introduction of colored persons for the purpose of education merely would seem to contemplate but a temporary residence, yet that class of people have seldom any settled establishment in their own state or inducements to return after the term of instruction has expired; and as their last association and attachments would be here; – a great portion of the whole number would make this state their permanent residence. The immense evils which such a mass of colored population would gather within this state when it has become their place of resort from other states and countries, would impose on our people burdens ..."
— Report of Committee Chairman Philip Pearl, Jr., to the May 1833 session of the Connecticut General Assembly

THE BLACK LAW

The "Black Law," as it came to be known, passed easily on May 16. The governor signed it on May 24.

> WHEREAS, attempts have been made to establish literary institutions in this state for the instruction of colored persons belonging to other states and countries, which would tend to the great increase of the colored population of the state, and thereby to the injury of the people : Therefore,
>
> SECT. 1. BE it enacted by the Senate and House of Representatives in General Assembly convened, That no person shall set up or establish in this state any school, academy, or literary institution, for the instruction or education of colored persons who are not inhabitants of this state, nor instruct or teach in any school, academy, or other literary institution whatsoever in this state, or harbor or board, for the purpose of attending or being taught or instructed in any such school, academy, or literary institution, any colored person who is not an inhabitant of any town in this state, without the consent, in writing, first obtained of a majority of the civil authority, and also of the select-men of the town in which such school, academy, or literary institution is situated ; and each and every person who shall knowingly do any act forbidden as aforesaid, or shall be aiding or assisting therein, shall, for the first offence, for-

The Black Law prohibited setting up a school for African-American students from outside Connecticut unless the town in which the school was located gave its approval. The punishment for violating the law was $100 for the first offense, $200 for the second, $400 for the third, and doubled again for each subsequent offense.

Out-of-state black students who attended an unauthorized school could be warned out under the existing law, although the provision for whipping offenders was removed.

"In 1833 when the law was passed ... it was celebrated by ringing the bell in the church ... and by firing a cannon 13 times, placed upon an elevation a few rods from my door ..."
— Prudence Crandall to Connecticut General Assembly, April, 1886

Rev. May and the Reverend Levi Kneeland, pastor of the Packerville Baptist Church to which Prudence belonged, came to the house to support Prudence and her students.

A month later, on June 27, 1833, Nehemiah Ensworth of Canterbury, father of one of Prudence's former white students, made a formal complaint that on June 24 Prudence Crandall and Almira Crandall had violated the Black Law.

"... Prudence Crandall of said Canterbury, wilfully and knowingly did instruct and teach ... certain colored persons, who at the time when so taught and instructed were not inhabitants of any town in this state ... without the consent in writing first had and obtained, of a majority of the civil authority and also the selectmen of said town of Canterbury ..."
— Complaint of Nehemiah Ensworth, grand juror of town of Canterbury, to Rufus Adams, justice of the peace, Windham, June 27, 1833

Sheriff's deputy George Cady delivered a writ for their arrest, then escorted the sisters before Justice of the Peace Rufus Adams, where Nehemiah Ensworth and Andrew Judson were also waiting.

JAIL

Although Prudence acknowledged that she maintained a school for African-American students in violation of the new Black Law, she nonetheless pleaded "not guilty." Charges against Almira were dismissed, for she was under the legal age of responsibility of 21.

Justice of the Peace Rufus Adams bound Prudence over for trial at the Windham County Court, to be held in August in Brooklyn. To avoid being jailed until her trial, Prudence was required to post a $150 bond. But she and her supporters had decided in advance not to pay the bond.

Prudence's enemies were shocked and disconcerted by this refusal; for a refined young woman to spend time in jail was "an outrage." But Sheriff Cady had no choice but to escort Prudence to the Windham County Courthouse in Brooklyn, the building on the far right in the illustration at right.

Prudence was put in a cell in the courthouse basement, close to the cell in which notorious murderer Oliver Watkins had been held before being hanged in 1831 for killing his wife. Her opponents contended that by her rebellious, unlawful activities Prudence had forfeited the special considerations normally accorded a woman.

EXPIRING MOMENTS OF MRS. WATKINS

"She has stepped out of the hallowed precincts of female propriety and now stands on common ground, and must expect common treatment."
— *Windham County Advertiser*, July 20, 1833

Prudence was joined in her cell by Anna Benson, sister of George Benson, Jr., one of Prudence's supporters. They spent the night behind bars. The next afternoon, their point having been made, George Benson posted bond and Prudence was released.

"Miss Crandall immured in [sic] a murderer's cell for the crime of teaching colored girls made a most vivid and startling impression upon the popular mind. Many who had before blamed her for disturbing the peace of Canterbury, were shocked at this alleged outrage . . . The story of her unjust imprisonment was noised in every direction, and unquestionably had great influence in awakening sympathy in her behalf and strengthening anti-slavery sentiment."
— Ellen Larned, *History of Windham County, Volume II*, 1880

While awaiting her trial in August, Prudence's enemies continued their campaign of intimidation and harassment. They tried to use the Black Law to pressure her family and friends into abandoning her.

"Mr. Crandall, if you go to your daughter's you are to be fined $100, for the first offense; $200 for the second, and double it every time; Mrs. Crandall, if you go there, you will be fined and your daughter Almira will be fined, and Mr. May and those gentlemen from Providence (Messrs. George and Henry Benson), if they come here they will be fined at the same rate. And your daughter, the one that established the school for colored females, will be taken up the same way as for stealing a horse, or for burglary. Her property will not be taken but she will be put in jail, not having the liberty of the yard. There is no mercy to be shown about it!"
— Andrew Judson and Rufus Adams to Pardon Crandall, June, 1833

The moment Judson and Adams left his house after delivering their message, Pardon Crandall, with characteristic contrariness, hitched up his wagon and defiantly headed for Prudence's school with some food – passing Andrew Judson on the way! The threats were never carried out.

Prudence initially told her opponents that her black students wouldn't worship at the First Congregational Church, for she would arrange for religious services to be conducted at the school. Concluding that that decision had been a mistake, she received permission from two members of the church's committee for her students to attend the Congregational church on the green.

Prudence was sick on the first Sabbath after permission had been granted. Almira escorted about a dozen black pupils to the church. The few seats at the rear of the building reserved for blacks couldn't accommodate all the students, so some sat in a vacant pew in the front. Several church members, outraged by what they considered an impudent affront, purchased the front pews and made sure their children occupied them the next Sabbath.

Thereafter, Prudence's Congregationalist students had to attend Westminster church, two miles from school. Some of the other students attended the Packerville Baptist Church, shown below. But soon they were barred from that house of worship by Daniel Packer, Jr., whose father, one of Prudence's supporters, was away on an extended trip.

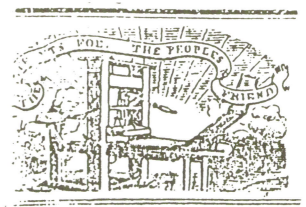

Newspapers throughout New England and New York, including *The Liberator*, had been reporting on the Canterbury controversy since its beginning. When the Norwich and Windham newspapers would no longer publish articles defending Prudence, Arthur Tappan gave Samuel May funds to start a newspaper. The weekly *Unionist* began publication on August 1, 1833.

"Finding that the little band with all its heroism was almost overborne by the storm of abuse and invective, and especially by misrepresentations which they were not allowed to rectify, Mr. [Arthur] Tappan made immediate arrangements for the publication of a newspaper in Brooklyn, 'to the advocacy of all human rights in general, and to the defence of the Canterbury school and its heroic teacher in particular.'"
— Ellen Larned, *History of Windham County, Volume II*, 1880

TRIAL

On August 23, 1833, Prudence went on trial at the Windham County Court. She pleaded "not guilty." Eight African-American students from the Canterbury Female Boarding School were subpoenaed as prosecution witnesses.

Prominent among the attorneys arguing the case against Prudence was none other than Andrew Judson. Fortunately, Prudence had a formidable trio of defense lawyers, retained by Arthur Tappan. They included William W. Ellsworth, a U.S. Congressman and son of one of the framers of the U.S. Constitution, Henry Strong, and Calvin Goddard. They accepted the case for a nominal fee.

Attorney William Ellsworth

More than a dozen witnesses were called to testify against Prudence in the second-floor courtroom with a Palladian window, shown right, overlooking the center of Brooklyn. Several students at first refused to testify on the grounds they might incriminate themselves, and did so only after warrants were issued for their arrest and confinement in jail if they didn't. The Reverend Levi Kneeland also refused to answer questions, and spent a night in jail before agreeing to testify.

The trial lasted two days, during which Prudence and several of her students spent the night at the home of George Benson in Brooklyn, shown below.

Defense attorney William Ellsworth wasted no time denying Prudence ran a school attended by African-American students from outside Connecticut. Instead he argued the greater issue – that blacks were American citizens, entitled to all the rights guaranteed by the United States Constitution in Article IV, Section 2, which declares "The citizens of each State shall be entitled to all privileges and immunities of citizens in the several States."

Ellsworth contended that because African Americans were citizens, the Black Law, by "prohibiting the citizens of other states from coming to this state to reside to pursue the acquisition of knowledge in a way open to the citizens of this state," was unconstitutional.

Prosecutor Andrew Judson responded by claiming that the word "citizens" in the U.S. Constitution "does not include colored persons." In addition to his legal arguments, he included an outrageous appeal to the jurors' fear.

"… let me allude merely to one other argument in support of this law, and that is the public safety. The southern states might emancipate their slaves and send them all to Connecticut instead of Liberia. The influx of that species of the population might be so great as to be overwhelming."
— Andrew Judson to Windham County Court jury, August 24, 1833

SECTION 2.
1. The citizens of each state shall be entitled to all privileges and immunities of citizens in the several states.

The fundamental issue of black citizenship was what made a trial in rural eastern Connecticut of compelling interest to people hundreds, even thousands of miles away. After deliberating for several hours, the jury of 12 white men was deadlocked, with seven members voting to convict and five to acquit. The case was continued until the next session of the Windham County Court in December.

Meanwhile, Canterbury citizens stepped up their intimidation. Animal dung was dumped down Prudence's well to foul it. Eggs and stones were thrown against her house, and on one occasion a large rock crashed through a window. Neighborhood boys sometimes followed Prudence and her students, blowing horns and beating drums to harass them. Dr. Andrew Harris twice refused to walk across the street to provide medical treatment for Prudence's students.

Andrew Judson managed to get Prudence's second trial moved up from December to October. Prudence's defense team had less than a week's notice of the change. They decided if Prudence were found guilty, they would appeal the verdict. Prudence was arrested a second time on September 26. This time two local men sympathetic to Prudence's cause posted bond to keep her out of jail.

At the second trial, on October 3, a plea of "not guilty" was again entered for Prudence. Andrew Judson was joined in his prosecution of the case by Chauncey F. Cleveland, a member of the Connecticut General Assembly and state's attorney for Windham County. Prudence was represented by Henry Strong and Calvin Goddard.

The presiding judge was David Daggett of New Haven, an eminent attorney and politician, a former United States Senator, and a member of the faculty at Yale Law School. Testimony and arguments from the first trial were read into evidence. This time, however, the outcome was far different. In his instructions to the jury, Daggett flatly declared that the Black Law "was constitutional; blacks not being citizens of the United States within the meaning of the Constitution." Following the judge's instructions, the jury returned a verdict of guilty. After her conviction, Prudence's lawyers "tendered a bill of exceptions to the charge of the Judge." Her appeal was scheduled for July of 1834 before the Supreme Court of Errors in Brooklyn.

Judge David Daggett

Chauncey F. Cleveland

The following nine months were eventful, bringing both joy and fear. There was cause for celebration on November 26, 1833, when a double wedding at the Westminster church united Sarah Harris and George Fayerweather, and Charles Harris and Mariah Davis in marriage.

Several months later, Prudence learned she had become an international heroine. From supporters in Great Britain she received letters and gifts, including a Staffordshire plate, shown above, illustrated with the image of an African and the Biblical text, "I am oppressed; undertake for me." The Ladies of Edinburgh Emancipation Society in Scotland sent Prudence a Bible "as a testimony of the estimation in which they hold your character and conduct."

> "No incident in the progress of the anti-slavery cause has stood out so prominently, either in this country or abroad, as the unmanly persecution of this heroic and philanthropic lady, for attempting to feed those who are famishing for the bread of knowledge. Especially in England has it attracted extraordinary attention …"
> — *The Liberator*, September 13, 1834

While Prudence awaited her appeals trial, tensions over race relations were flaring into violence in the Northeast. Riots broke out in New York, Philadelphia, and even in nearby Norwich, Connecticut. Abolitionist speakers were harassed and assaulted in Middletown.

Harassment of Prudence grew uglier. In the summer of 1834, Prudence found a dead black-and-white cat, its throat slit, hanging by its neck on her gate.

On January 28, 1834, Frederick Olney of Norwich, an African-American man who was an agent for *The Liberator*, came to Prudence's school to visit Mariah and Charles Harris. While Olney was there, a fire was discovered in a corner of Prudence's house. The alarm was sounded, and a number of townspeople responded — no matter how much they despised the Canterbury Female Boarding School, a fire in one house could easily spread to others if not quickly brought under control.

Frederick Olney was instrumental in putting out the fire, which was suspected, but never proven, to have been arson. Prudence's enemies cynically tried to use the incident to discredit her by charging Olney with setting the fire. At his trial in March of 1834, the jury required just 15 minutes to find Olney innocent.

UNEXPECTED ROMANCE

In a startling, unexpected development, Prudence found herself being courted by the Reverend Calvin Philleo, a Baptist minister she first met when he attended her trial in August of 1833. Philleo, 46, was a recent widower with three children, two still at home. He apparently had decided to marry Prudence before ever laying eyes on her, and actually proposed marriage the first time they met.

Calvin Philleo was a man of questionable character, described by two fellow Baptist ministers as "very eccentric." Rumor said his indiscretions had included literally advertising for a new wife even as he was engaged to another woman. Another time he intended to propose marriage to a woman he had met only once – until he learned she was already married.

Prudence's friends were disturbed by stories they'd heard about Calvin Philleo. They frankly told her about the rumors, their own negative impressions of Philleo, and their reservations about the marriage.

Prudence herself wasn't sure what she felt or ought to do. At times she was completely in love with Calvin; at others she felt she should end the relationship. But by March of 1834 Prudence and Calvin Philleo were engaged to be married.

LEGAL APPEAL

Prudence didn't attend her appeals trial when it opened on July 18 in Brooklyn. Ellsworth and Goddard put forth the same straightforward, yet highly explosive, arguments that Rev. Samuel May had first expressed back in March of 1833, and that Ellsworth had presented at Prudence's first trial. Andrew Judson repeated his contention that blacks were not citizens, and thus not entitled to Constitutional protections.

The Supreme Court of Errors issued its judgement from the State House in Hartford, shown at left. It reversed Prudence's conviction, but on a minor technicality that was one of two points on which Prudence's attorneys had based their appeal: "insufficiency of information." That referred to the conviction's failure to include the allegation that the school had been established without the "license of the civil authority and selectmen" of Canterbury.

The Supreme Court of Errors carefully pointed that it "did not decide either of the points presented by the counsel" — meaning its reversal of the verdict against Prudence was not intended to be a stand for or against black citizenship. The fundamental issue raised by Prudence Crandall's school remained unresolved for more than 20 years, until the United State Supreme Court issued its historic Dred Scott v. Sanford decision in 1857.

CHAPTER TWELVE
When All Else Failed
TURNING TO THE TACTICS OF TERROR

The government could have continued prosecuting Prudence Crandall. But within two months that was a moot issue.

Prudence's enemies kept up their campaign of ill will following the appeals court decision. When she and Calvin Philleo decided to marry on August 12, Prudence's pastor, the Reverend Levi Kneeland of the Packerville Baptist Church, was on his deathbed and unable to officiate. Prudence and Calvin asked the new pastor of the Canterbury Congregational Church, the Reverend Otis Whiton, to marry them at her house. But on the day of the wedding, Rev. Whiton received an anonymous donation of money to his church, given on the condition that he not perform the marriage.

Prudence Crandall and Calvin Philleo were wed in Brooklyn by the Congregational minister, Reverend Tillotson. Less than a month after their marriage, the anger, fear, resentment, and frustration that had been simmering in Canterbury for more than a year and a half boiled over.

"… the minister of the church refused to step into my house and perform the marriage ceremony … He was invited some days before hand but did not refuse till the very set hour. He then sent in a not[e] sayin[g] he could not officiate."

— Prudence Crandall to Ellen Larned, July 2, 1869

Impatient with the law's failure to close Prudence's school, shown at left, some Canterbury residents decided to take matters into their own hands. Late on September 9, 1834, Prudence and Calvin and about 20 students awoke to discover a crowd of what *The Liberator* called "midnight ruffians" attacking the house, depicted in the highly dramatized illustration above. Armed with lead pipes and wooden clubs the mob smashed windows and broke into the house, ransacking the ground floor, rendering the two front rooms almost uninhabitable. Prudence, Calvin, and her students feared for their lives.

MISS CRANDALL'S SCHOOL ABANDONED.

Human endurance has its bounds, and the requirements of duty have theirs. By the following Advertisements, which we copy from the Brooklyn Unionist, it appears that another cowardly attack has been made upon Miss Crandall's (now Mrs. Phileo's) dwelling, by some midnight ruffians in Canterbury, and that it has been deemed advisable to abandon the school in that heathenish village, and to let ANDREW T. JUDSON and his associates, with the whole State of Connecticut, have all the infamy and guilt which attach to the violent suppression of so praiseworthy an institution. O, tempora! O, mores!

$50 REWARD!! — During the night of Tuesday the 9th inst. about 12 o'clock, the house of the subscriber in Canterbury was assaulted by a number of lawless persons with heavy clubs or iron bars; five window sashes were destroyed, and more than ninety panes of glass were dashed to pieces, and the family greatly alarmed.

The above named reward is hereby offered to any one, who will give information that will lead to the detection of the perpetrators of the outrage, or any one of them. CALVIN PHILEO.
Canterbury, Sept. 11, 1834.

FOR SALE. The house in Canterbury occupied by the late Prudence Crandall, now the wife of the subscriber. The impunity with which repeated assaults have been made upon these premises, has awakened the apprehension that the property, and perhaps the lives of those connected with the school, are insecure. I have therefore thought it proper, and do hereby advertise the house and appurtenances thereof for sale.

For further particulars inquire of the subscriber, or of
PARDON CRANDALL of *Canterbury*, or
SAMUEL J. MAY of *Brooklyn*.
CALVIN PHILEO.
Canterbury, Sept. 11, 1834.

For Prudence, the terrifying mob attack was the last straw. Unwilling to further risk her safety or that of her students, she took the advice offered by her husband, father, brother Hezekiah, and even her staunch supporter Samuel May, and closed the Canterbury Female Boarding School permanently.

Prudence asked Samuel May to break the bad news to her students.

"The words [telling the black students that the Canterbury school would close] almost blistered my lips. My heart glowed with indignation. I felt ashamed of Canterbury, ashamed of Connecticut, ashamed of my country."
— Rev. Samuel May, *The Liberator*, Sept. 20, 1834

In a bittersweet bit of irony, Sarah Harris Fayerweather gave birth to her first child on September 9, 1834. She named the girl *Prudence Crandall Fayerweather.*

Calvin Phileo advertised in *The Unionist* and *The Liberator* for information about those who had attacked the house, but got no response.

The house was advertised for sale in *The Unionist* and *The Liberator* — by Calvin, who, as Prudence's husband of barely two months, was legally empowered to dispose of her property with or without her consent. The property was sold on November 15, 1834, for the same amount Prudence paid for it three years earlier. The deed transferring the property was signed by both Prudence and Calvin.

Chapter Thirteen
In The Whirlwind's Wake
Exile, Tribulation, and Vindication

THE CRANDALLS

The next decade was one of tragedy and sorrow for the Crandall family. Much of their misfortune was the result of the bigoted backlash against Prudence's pioneering school for African-American girls.

Almira Crandall, described by William Lloyd Garrison as "a very beautiful girl," married John Rand, a teacher, and moved to New York City. But she returned to Canterbury when she fell ill. She died there in 1837, at the age of 24.

Dr. Reuben Crandall became an unwitting victim of the hatred for his sister's school. In 1835 he moved to Washington, D.C., a Southern city, where slavery was legal and abolitionists abhorred. He took with him some abolitionist publications and issues of *The Liberator*.

A neighbor borrowed some of Reuben's abolitionist materials, which fell into the hands of Francis Scott Key, the district attorney for the District of Columbia and author of the words to the "Star-Spangled Banner." On August 10, 1835, Key had Reuben jailed on charges of "seditious libel" – distribution of materials encouraging slaves and free blacks to rise up against their oppressors.

Public opinion against abolitionists ran so high in the nation's capital that friends and relatives were afraid to visit Reuben or even try to raise his outrageously high bail of $5,000. Reuben's lawyers got the trial delayed until emotions could cool.

"As my family was the setters up of that school, and myself, a supporter of my family, if I should come to your assistance I should be taken by Lynch law and perhaps be tied up by the neck without judge or jury."
— Pardon Crandall to Reuben Crandall, January 25, 1836

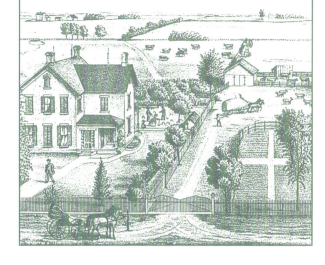

Pardon Crandall decided to join the exodus from Connecticut. In 1837 he went to the frontier settlement of Troy Grove, Illinois, shown above, to prepare his new property for his family's move.

"I have swapped away my farm in Canterbury for six hundred acres of land in the state of Illinois. I shall settle my affairs as soon as I can and go into the wilderness to seek any assylom [sic] or hiding place from the turmoils and contentions of this world and find a place to lay my weary and decrepit bones."
— Pardon Crandall to Prudence Crandall

Reuben Crandall finally went on trial in April of 1836. Francis Scott Key, calling seditious libel an act of treason, asked for the death penalty. Reuben was found not guilty. But nine months in the Washington jail had aggravated his chronic lung problems. Reuben sailed for Jamaica, where he hoped the gentler weather would improve his health — and where he died on January 17, 1838.

Francis Scott Key

In Illinois Pardon Crandall contracted malaria. He managed to return to Canterbury on June 2, 1838. He died seven weeks later. On July 20, the day after Pardon's death, Hezekiah Crandall's wife, Clarissa Cornell Crandall, died suddenly. She left Hezekiah with six children, including the baby she had borne just 12 days earlier.

Sadly, Prudence's marriage to Calvin Philleo proved unhappy almost from the start. Calvin was an impulsive, irresponsible, cantankerous, often cruel man, whom many considered mentally unstable or incompetent. He controlled all of Prudence's property and money, which he managed poorly. He treated Prudence like an incompetent child, which was particularly galling for the bright, well-educated, independent woman.

"… my husband opposed me, more than anyone. He would not let me read the books that he himself read, but I did read them. I read all sides and searched for the truth, whether it was in science, religion, or humanity."

— Prudence Crandall to George Thayer, *Pedal and Path*, 1887

Although Prudence and Calvin had no children of their own, Prudence was a devoted stepmother to Calvin's children from his first marriage. They returned her affection.

Calvin and Prudence moved to upstate New York in 1834 and returned to Canterbury in 1840. Prudence's marriage to Calvin deteriorated into a chaotic series of moves, separations, and attempts to reconcile motivated primarily by Prudence's sense of duty and usually doomed to failure by Calvin's erratic behavior. Calvin managed to lose whatever funds they had, and the family frequently lived in poverty. In 1844 Calvin's children sought to have a legal conservator named for him, declaring "that said Calvin Philleo is now an insane person."

In 1842, deciding she could no longer tolerate life with Calvin, Prudence moved to Pardon's Illinois property, accompanied only by her brother Hezekiah's teenage son. In 1843 Esther Crandall joined her daughter in Illinois. Prudence visited Canterbury in 1847, then returned to Illinois where she lived in the house shown above. She would never see Connecticut again.

Prudence became the matriarch of an ever-changing and growing extended family that included her stepchildren, stepgrandchildren, nieces, and nephews, and their spouses. She farmed, taught school, did whatever was necessary to put food on the table. Calvin would appear unannounced in Illinois to live with the family in whichever of the several houses they were occupying, disrupting their lives with his eccentricities and bullying, then disappear again on some wild venture.

Whether Prudence ever seriously considered legally ending her marriage is not known. Calvin's own daughter thought her stepmother would be more than justified if she decided to divorce Calvin. But Prudence remained Calvin's wife, caring for and supporting him, on and off, for decades.

THE LIFE AND LEGACY OF PRUDENCE CRANDALL

Despite her personal difficulties, Prudence remained committed to the on-going struggle for abolitionism and civil rights for blacks, as well as to religious issues, politics, the crusade for women's rights and suffrage, and temperance. She wrote and spoke about these topics. She followed the rise of Abraham Lincoln of Illinois to the presidency in 1860, the Civil War that erupted in 1861 and ended four years later, and the complete abolition of slavery by the Thirteenth Amendment to the U.S. Constitution in 1865.

The ratification of the Fourteenth Amendment to the U.S. Constitution in 1868 guaranteed citizenship to African Americans. It settled the civil rights issue that Prudence had been one of the first to raise to public attention with her school more than 30 years earlier.

The Journey of Prudence Crandall

Hezekiah had barely arrived in Illinois when Prudence decided to trade her property there for a farm in Elk Falls, Kansas. They moved to Kansas in 1877. It was the last stop in Prudence's 40-year sometimes voluntary, sometimes involuntary exile from Connecticut.

Esther Crandall died in 1872 in Illinois. Two years later, Calvin Philleo died there as well. His death ended four decades of marital misery with which Prudence had coped gallantly, often supporting and caring for her husband out of a sense of duty.

Hezekiah Crandall had re-married in 1839, the year after his first wife's death. His new wife, Almira Clapp Burgess, bore him four children. After her death in 1851, Hezekiah married again. When he buried his third wife in 1876, Hezekiah left Connecticut to live with Prudence, with whom many of his children were already residing.

In 1877, Sarah Harris Fayerweather made the long trip from Rhode Island to Kansas to visit her former teacher. The reunion of the two crusaders for equal rights lasted several weeks. Sarah Fayerweather returned to Rhode Island, where she died the following year. Hezekiah Crandall died in Elk Falls in 1881.

Very late in life Prudence enjoyed personal vindication for the controversial stand she had taken more than 50 years earlier. In 1885, John S. Smith of Central Village, Connecticut, visited Prudence in Kansas to tell her that some Canterbury residents were petitioning the Connecticut General Assembly to make restitution for her persecution under the Black Law.

Prudence, now past 80, was living in a tiny, crudely furnished three-room house. Her dresses consisted of a piece of cloth in which she cut a hole for her head, then tied around the waist as shown in this 1874 photograph.

VINDICATION

"For over fifty years this disgrace has remained on our state … If justice is to be done, even at this late date, it should not be long delayed, for Prudence Crandall in the natural order of things, has not long to live." — Hartford Times, 1886

The General Assembly moved cautiously in considering the petition; Prudence, after all, had been brought to trial for violating the Black Law, although her guilt was never established in court and the law was repealed in 1838. The General Assembly's Appropriations Committee initially rejected the proposal. But powerful public opinion in Prudence's favor, fostered by coverage in local newspapers as well as those in Boston and New York, and even a petition from more than 100 Canterbury residents, persuaded them to change their minds.

"We, the undersigned citizens of this State and of the town of Canterbury, mindful of the dark blot that rests upon our fair fame and name for the cruel outrages inflicted upon a former citizen of our Commonwealth, a noble Christian woman, Miss Prudence Crandall … respectfully pray your Honorable Body to make … late reparations for the wrong done her …"

— Petition of Citizens of Canterbury to the Connecticut General Assembly, 1886

"I shall never plead poverty … My plea will be for justice … When a state has falsely imprisoned an innocent citizen and passed unconstitutional laws by which they are harassed and property destroyed it [is] right they should compensate the abused … I feel that it is a duty I owe myself and also to the State to ask for redress for such slander and abuse as I have received at their hands."

– Prudence Crandall to John S. Smith, Central Village Connecticut, Nov. 3, 1885

Helping spur the General Assembly to act in Prudence's favor was a movement to purchase her former home/school in Canterbury as a matter of "poetic justice," and have her return to spend her remaining years in it. One of those behind this effort was Mark Twain, a resident of Hartford, Connecticut.

Prudence wrote Twain declining the generous gesture to restore her to her former home. For the rest of her life she treasured copies of his books and a photograph of himself, shown at left, that Twain sent her.

On April 2, 1886, almost 53 years to the day from when she had formally opened her school for black students in Canterbury, Prudence received a telegram with the news that the General Assembly, meeting in the new State Capitol in Hartford, shown above, had approved a pension of $400 a year for life for her.

The pension enabled Prudence to buy a better house in Elk Falls, shown at left. She continued to read and speak on a wide variety of subjects, including spiritualism, temperance, and other reforms. To the end she lived the often lonely life of a relentless, fearless seeker of the truth.

Prudence died in 1890, at the age of 87, of respiratory problems. She was buried beside her brother Hezekiah in Kansas, half a continent away from the Connecticut village where she made her stand for racial equality that was an early landmark in the history of American civil rights.

In 1969, Prudence Crandall's house in Canterbury was purchased by the State of Connecticut. In 1984, Connecticut Governor William O'Neill dedicated Prudence Crandall's house as a museum operated by the Connecticut Historical Commission, now the Historic Preservation and Museum Division of the Connecticut Commission on Arts, Tourism, Culture, History and Film. The Prudence Crandall Museum in 1991 was designated a National Historic Landmark. In 1995, the Connecticut General Assembly designated Prudence Crandall Connecticut's official state heroine.

"I read all sides, and searched for the truth whether it was in science, religion, or humanity … No one visits me, and I begin to think they are afraid of me. I think the ministers are afraid I shall upset their religious beliefs, and advise the members of their congregation not to call on me, but I don't care."

— Prudence Crandall to George Thayer, *Pedal and Path*, 1887

The Students

The fates of many of the black girls who attended the Canterbury Female Boarding School remain to be determined. But several are known to have become women whose accomplishments reflected well on the education they received at Prudence Crandall's school.

Sarah Harris Fayerweather

and her husband, George Fayerweather, lived in New London until 1855, after which they moved to Kingston, Rhode Island, and lived in the house shown below. They were active abolitionists, whose visitors included William Lloyd Garrison and Frederick Douglass. The couple became conductors on the Underground Railroad, helping fugitive slaves on the route north to freedom. George Fayerweather died in 1869. In 1877 Sarah made the long journey to Kansas to visit her former schoolteacher, with whom she had made history. Sarah died in 1878.

Mary Harris

Sarah Harris's sister, married Pelluman Williams of Norwich in 1845. Pelluman Williams was vice president of the 1849 Connecticut Convention of Colored Men. The family lived in Norwich, where Pelluman Williams was a teacher, until the early 1860s when they moved to Louisiana. Mary and Pelluman Williams were both alive in 1881, still teaching black children and adults.

After Prudence's school closed, **Julia Williams** of Boston went to the Noyes Academy in New Canaan, New Hampshire, which in 1835 met the same fate as the Canterbury Female Boarding School. Williams was an outspoken advocate of abolition and African-American rights. She attended the Anti-Slavery Convention in New York in 1837 as a delegate from Boston, and in 1839 signed a petition to the Massachusetts legislature opposing legislation banning interracial marriage. Julia Williams married Henry Highland Garnett, shown at right, a fugitive slave she first met at the Noyes Academy. Garnett, who had acquired an education in New York, became a minister. He was also one of the most prominent black abolitionists, and his wife participated in his crusade. Julia and Henry Garnett traveled to London, and in 1852 to Jamaica, where Julia headed a Female Industrial School. After the Civil War Julia helped freedmen in Washington, D.C. Julia Williams Garnett died in 1870 in Pittsburgh. "She literally wore herself out in the service of God and her people," according to her obituary in the *Christian Reporter* newspaper, shown at right.

> Mrs. Julia Williams Garnet, the beloved wife of the Rev. Henry Highland Garnett, Prest. of Avery College, departed this life suddenly at her late residence in Allegheny City, Pa., at twenty minutes past 12 o'clock, A.M., Friday, Jan. 7th, 1870. . . . From a child Mrs. Garnet thirsted for education, and she was one of the scholars of the famous seminary of Miss Prudence Crandall, at Canterbury, Conn., and remained there until that school was broken up by pro-slavery violence and Miss Crandall was thrown in jail for the crime of teach[ing]. . . . Having qualified herself [she was] appointed to a school [where she taught] for several years, and wa[s ...] [Rev.] Henry Highland Gar[nett ...] of her husband in his m[inistry ...] West Indies, as the f[...] Master in ministering [...] [freed]men in Washington, and ob[...] the lamented Hon. Edw[... on her] behalf, she exemplified in her lif[e ...] [no]ble Christian woman. He[r ...] [anti-]slavery cause, and her sacrific[es ...] may not be recorded [...]

Opponents

"I could weep tears of blood for the part I took in this matter. I now regard it as utterly abominable." — Philip Pearl, Jr., 1838

Andrew Judson, Prudence Crandall's most venomous, relentless persecutor, became a judge, and not long after sat in judgement of a group of Africans kidnapped from their homeland, who were on trial for seizing control of the *Amistad*, the ship carrying them to slavery in Cuba. Judson surprised everyone when he decided in favor of the Africans.

State's Attorney **Chauncey Cleveland**, who helped prosecute Prudence Crandall, was elected governor of Connecticut in 1842, and returned to that office in 1843 and 1844. In 1849, he was elected to represent Connecticut in the United States House of Representatives, and re-elected to a second term two years later. He died in 1887.

Judge David Daggett in 1834 concluded a distinguished 48-year legal and political career that had included election to the United States Senate and helping found the Yale Law School. He died in 1851.

State Senator **Phillip Pearl, Jr.**, of Hampton, whose daughter Hannah attended Prudence's school when the student body was all white, had written the Black Law. But Pearl soon became a convert to abolitionism. In 1838 he was vice president of the Connecticut Anti-Slavery Society, and helped fugitive slaves to freedom via the Underground Railroad.

Eliza Glasko of Griswold married John Peterson, who was a prominent black educator in New York City for more than half a century. Peterson was also deacon of St. Philip's Church, a black Episcopal congregation. Eliza Glasko Peterson reportedly died in 1874.

Harriet Lanson of New Haven hoped to become a teacher of black students or perhaps a missionary. But she never had a chance to realize her dreams. Having survived an early childhood of poverty and neglect, she died of tuberculosis in New Haven in 1835, at the age of 18.

Ann Eliza Hammond may have returned to live in Providence. She was still alive in 1871, when Sarah Harris Fayerweather wrote to Prudence that Ann was going to England.

Elizabeth N. Smith returned to her hometown of Providence, where she was a teacher, and later principal, of a school for black students. In later life she gave private lessons, and was known as a talented pianist and fine linguist. She died sometime after 1865.

Mariah Davis married Charles Harris, brother of Sarah Harris, in 1833. She and Charles lived at 30 Cedar Street in Norwich, where Charles operated a restaurant.

Other African-American students at the Canterbury Female Boarding School whose fates are as yet unknown include:

Henrietta Bolt, New York City
Elizabeth Douglass Bustill, Philadelphia
M.E. Carter, New York City
Jerusha Congdon, New York City
Theodosia Degrass, New York City
Amy Fenner
Polly Freeman, New York City
Sarah Lloyd Hammond, Providence
Elizabeth Henly, Philadelphia
J.K. Johnson, Philadelphia
Ann Peterson, New York City
Mariah Robinson, Providence
Catherine Ann Weldon, New York City
Eliza Weldon
Ann Elizabeth Wilder/Wiles, New York City
Emila Wilson

Supporters

William Lloyd Garrison continued his radical abolitionist activities, including publication of *The Liberator*, until 1865, when the Thirteenth Amendment to the United States Constitution outlawed slavery. But Garrison continued to crusade for other reforms, including women's suffrage, until his death in 1879 at the age of 73.

The Reverend Samuel May persevered as an anti-slavery activist, and served as a conductor on the Underground Railroad helping fugitive slaves to freedom. Rev. May left Brooklyn, Connecticut, in 1836, for pastorates in Massachusetts and New York. He embraced many other reforms, including universal peace, temperance, improvement of public education, and equal rights for women. He died in 1871 at the age of 73.

Prudence's primary defense attorney, **William Ellsworth**, was elected governor of Connecticut in 1838, and re-elected to three one-year terms. He was later appointed judge of the Connecticut Supreme Court of Errors. He died in 1868 at the age of 76.

The Reverend Simeon Jocelyn left his pastorate of the African church in New Haven in 1834, but continued working for abolition and civil rights. His crusade incited a mob to attack his home in 1837. Undaunted, Jocelyn became an agent on the Underground Railroad, and helped create an integrated neighborhood in New Haven.

Arthur Tappan continued his opposition to slavery in a variety of ways, including funding other abolitionist newspapers and assisting fugitive slaves. He provided major financial assistance toward the founding of Oberlin College in Ohio, the first college in the United States to admit African-American students. Tappan died in 1865 at the age of 79.

Chapter Fourteen
"To All On Equal Terms"
The Legacy of Prudence Crandall and the Canterbury Female Boarding School

The issue the Connecticut Supreme Court of Errors chose to sidestep in 1834 – whether blacks were citizens – was finally addressed by the U.S. Supreme Court in 1857 in the case of Dred Scott v. Sanford. Dred Scott was a slave who sued for his freedom on the basis that his owner had taken him to live for a time in a free state. The U.S. Supreme Court decided against Scott. In the "Opinion of the Court," Chief Justice Roger Taney declared that under the U.S. Constitution blacks "had no rights which the white man was bound to respect." Taney cited evidence and opinion presented at Prudence Crandall's second trial 24 years earlier in support of the decision. The Dred Scott case added fuel to the already blazing controversy over slavery and black civil rights that would erupt into the Civil War four years later.

". . . Chief Justice Dagget, before whom the [Prudence Crandall] case was tried, held that persons of that description [African Americans] were not citizens of a State, within the meaning of the word citizen in the Constitution of the United States. . . . from the early hostility it [Connecticut] displayed to the slave trade on the coast of Africa, we may expect to find the laws of that State as lenient and favorable to the subject race as those of any other State in the Union; and if we find that at the time the Constitution was adopted, they were not even there raised to the rank of citizens, but were still held and treated as property, and the laws relating to them passed with reference altogether to the interest and convenience of the white race, we shall hardly find them elevated to a higher rank anywhere else."

— Dred Scott v. Sanford, Opinion of the Court, 1857

The prosecution of Prudence Crandall was still having an impact on civil rights activism nearly a century later. The argument made at her appeals trial by William Ellsworth and Henry Goddard was cited in arguments in the landmark 1954 Brown v. Board of Education case, in which the U.S. Supreme Court declared the practice of "separate but equal" public schools for whites and blacks unconstitutional.

"The Ellsworth-Goddard argument is one of the classic statements of the social case for equality of opportunity irrespective of race. It gave immense impetus to the emerging concept of American nationality and citizenship. Fully reported and widely circulated as a tract, it soon became one of the fountainheads of anti-slavery constitutional theory. It figured prominently in Abolitionist writings throughout the 'thirties."

— Arguments, Brown v. Board of Education, 1954

THE LIFE AND LEGACY OF PRUDENCE CRANDALL

Prudence Crandall's portrait is included on the "American National Tree" in the National Constitution Center in Philadelphia.

Prudence Crandall, her African-American students, and their supporters had taken a bold, courageous, early stand in support of equal educational opportunity and, by extension, full civil rights for blacks. But the significance of their actions transcends any one issue.

Crandall and her young black pupils lived in a society that denied them most rights and opportunities modern women take for granted. Their culture considered women inferior to men, and believed their only true and acceptable destiny was to marry a man to whom they would be subservient, for whom they would make a home and bear children. For African Americans the situation was even worse, for there were many who believed them to be a sub-human species whose proper fate was to serve the whites who were their superiors.

But these women and girls, rendered nearly powerless by their society, had the conscience, the courage, and the determination to take a stand against racism, sexism, and injustice. They risked everything, including their lives. Their significant contribution toward making rights and liberties expressed in the Declaration of Independence and the United States Constitution a reality for African Americans and for women of all races is their enduring legacy.

CHAPTER FIFTEEN

Sites in Eastern Connecticut Associated with the Prudence Crandall Episode

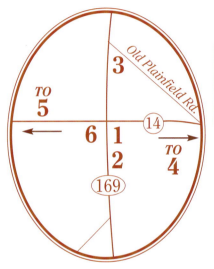

CANTERBURY

1
Dr. Andrew Harris House*

2
First Congregational Church (Original built in 1805, replacement built in 1964)

3
Jedidiah Shepard House*

4
Packerville Baptist Church

5
Westminster Congregational Church

6
Prudence Crandall Museum

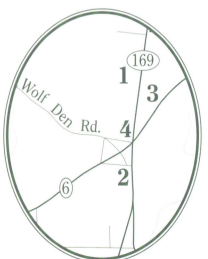

BROOKLYN

1
Rev. Samuel May House*

2
Brooklyn Unitarian Church

3
George Benson House*

4
Brooklyn Town Hall (formerly Windham County Courthouse and Jail)

Buildings marked with an asterisk (*) are private. All others are accessible to the public.

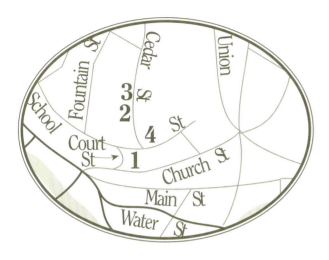

NORWICH

1
Beulah Land
Church of God
in Christ

2
Charles and
Mariah
Harris
House*

3
William
Harris
House*

4
Norwich Female
Academy*

The Jail Hill section of Norwich became a neighborhood of modestly prosperous African-American homeowners during the 1830s and 1840s. Several residents had ties to the Canterbury Female Boarding School.

Around 1836 Charles Harris, brother of Sarah Harris, built a house at 30 Cedar Street. Here Charles, who operated a restaurant, lived with his wife, Mariah Davis.

Next door at 34 Cedar Street, Charles and Sarah Harris's brother William H. Harris built a house around 1848. William worked as a ship's cook.

The Norwich Female Academy was built on Jail Hill in 1828. Whether Sarah Harris ever sought admission to this impressive private school in her home town is unknown. But when Sarah's family moved to Canterbury, and she learned of her friend Mariah's arrangement with Prudence Crandall, she seized the rare opportunity to obtain the education she needed to herself become a teacher to young African Americans.

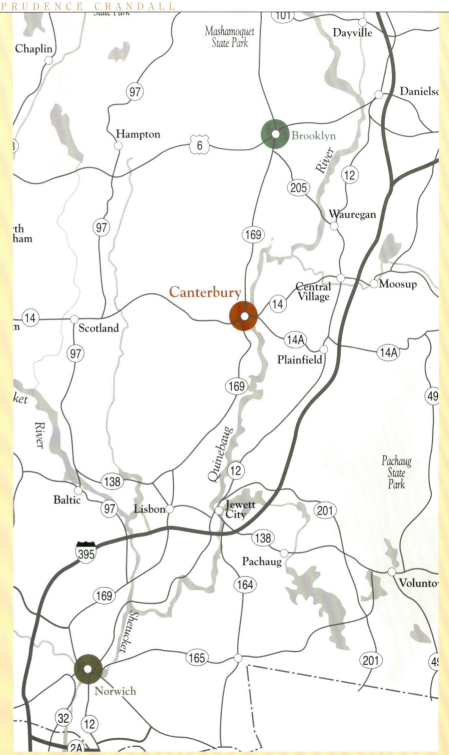

Illustration Identification and Credits/Selected Bibliography

Each page number is in bold, followed by identification and credit information for images that appear on that page.

Abbreviations for Institutions
CHS The Connecticut Historical Society, Hartford, Connecticut
CSL Connecticut State Library, Hartford, Connecticut
DRM Diana Ross McCain, photographer
GML Godfrey Memorial Library, Middletown, Connecticut
MCH Museum of Connecticut History, Connecticut State Library, Hartford, Connecticut
MCHS Middlesex County Historical Society, Middletown, Connecticut
PCM The Prudence Crandall Museum, Canterbury, Connecticut

PROLOGUE
1 Prudence Crandall, copy by Carl Henry of portrait painted in 1833 by Francis Alexander, original at Cornell University, Ithaca, NY, PCM; "Colored Schools Broken Up in the Free States," *Anti-Slavery Almanac*, 1839, PCM.

CHAPTER ONE
Shake-up in the Land of Steady Habits: Connecticut and Canterbury in the 1830s
2 *Connecticut Courant*, March 17, 1817, CSL; *Map of Connecticut from Actual Survey*, Hartford, CT: Willis Thrall, 1831, CHS.
3 Portrait of Governor Oliver Wolcott, Jr., by George F. Wright, MCH; "South View of the Churches in Bridgeport," *Connecticut Historical Collections*, by John Warner Barber, New Haven: 1836.
4 Detail of *Map of the United States*, by Eleazer Huntington, New York: E. Strong, 1835, CHS; "Emigration in 1817," *Recollections of a Lifetime, Volume II*, by Samuel Griswold Goodrich, New York: 1856.
5 *Connecticut Courant*, Oct. 17, 1817, CSL; "Western view of Danielsonville, Killingly," *Connecticut Historical Collections*, by John Warner Barber, New Haven: 1836; photograph of house on Canterbury Green, DRM.

CHAPTER TWO
Rebellion in the Blood: Prudence Crandall and The Crandall Family
6 Prudence Crandall, copy of portrait painted in 1833 by Francis Alexander, PCM; detail of sampler worked by Prudence Crandall, circa 1812, PCM; Esther Crandall, PCM.
7 Moses Brown, from *Centennial History of the Moses Brown School*, by Rayner Wickersham Kelsey, Providence: 1919; New England Yearly Meeting School circa 1831, from *Centennial History of the Moses Brown School*, by Rayner Wickersham Kelsey, Providence: 1919; "Am I not a Man and a Brother?," CSL; Hezekiah Crandall, 1874, PCM; "View of Plainfield," *Connecticut Historical Collections*, by John Warner Barber, New Haven: 1836; diploma of Reuben Crandall, Yale University, 1828, PCM; Packerville Baptist Church, PCM.

CHAPTER THREE
Only Three R's - Except for the Rich: Public and Private Education in Early Nineteenth-Century Connecticut
8 Detail from cover of *Catalogue of the Pupils of Isaac Webb and Julius S. Shailer's Family School, Maple Grove, Middletown, Conn.*, 1841, MCHS; "Aunt Delight," *Recollections of a Lifetime*, by Samuel Griswold Goodrich, New York: 1856; Nathan Hale schoolhouse, circa 1750, East Haddam, Connecticut, DRM.
9 Detail of page from *Grammatical Institute of the English Language, Pt. I* [commonly known as the "blue-backed speller"], by Noah Webster, Hartford: 1783, CHS; *Annual Catalogue of the Hartford Female Seminary*, Hartford: 1835, CSL; "Yale College," *Connecticut Historical Collections*, by John Warner Barber, New Haven: 1836.

CHAPTER FOUR
A Golden Opportunity: The Canterbury Female Boarding School, 1831-32
10 Prudence Crandall House, PCM.
11 Detail from account book of Stephen Coit, Canterbury, Connecticut, CHS; students' bedroom, Prudence Crandall Museum, DRM.
12 "Lesson XXXII. Habitations - Shells - Pearls - Habits," "Lesson XII. Mammalia of the Sea," "Lesson XXVIII. Habits of Insects - Carpenter Ants - Bees," *The Class Book of Nature*, edited by J. Frost, Hartford: 1843, CSL; "Columbus Discovers America," "Eastern Hemisphere," *Peter Parley's Method of Telling About Geography To Children*, Hartford: 1829, CHS; astronomy chart, *The Geography of the Heavens*, by E.H. Burritt, Hartford: 1833, CSL.

CHAPTER FIVE
"To Get a Little More Learning": A Student of Color Seeks Admission
13 Sarah Harris Fayerweather, circa 1860s, PCM; *The Liberator* masthead, 1831; "Am I Not a Woman and a Sister?," *The Liberator*, 1831.
14 Jedidiah Shepard house, DRM; sampler attributed to Sarah Harris, circa 1826-1828, courtesy of Ralph and Glee Krueger; detail of *Norwich from the West Side of the River*, by Fitz Hugh Lane, 1849, CHS; Beulah Land Church of God in Christ, Norwich, Connecticut, DRM.

CHAPTER SIX
No Small Courage: Two Women Stand Up for the Right to an Education
15 Historical interpreter Kimberly Dysart in character as Prudence Crandall, photographed at Prudence Crandall Museum, 2003, DRM.

CHAPTER SEVEN
"Truly This is Our Home": The History of Connecticut's Black Community
16 "The First, Second, and Last Scenes of Mortality," silk on linen needlework, by Prudence Punderson, Preston, Connecticut, circa 1783, CHS; Bill of sale for "Mary a black woman and her child Tobe," sold by Eliphalet Nott to Samuel Mather for $200, February 1, 1808, MCHS.
17 "TEN DOLLARS REWARD," *Connecticut Courant*, July 5, 1774, CHS; Venture Smith gravestone, East Haddam Cemetery, East Haddam, Connecticut, DRM; "Rev. Lemuel Haynes, A.M.," *Sketches of the Life and Character of the Rev. Lemuel Haynes*, by Timothy Mather Cooley, 1837, CHS.
18 "An Act to Prevent Slavery," *Public Statute Laws of the State of Connecticut...1835*, Hartford: 1835; "Qualifications of Electors," *Constitution of the State of Connecticut*, 1818, *Public Statute Laws of the State of Connecticut...1835*, Hartford: 1835; portrait of Nancy Toney, circa 1850, private collection; James Mars, from *History of Norfolk, Litchfield County, Connecticut*, by Theron Wilmot Crissey, Everett, MA: 1900.
19 "Colored Persons," *Wells' (formerly Bolles) City Directory for Hartford. 1848*, Hartford: 1848, GML; detail of map of Griswold, *Atlas of New London County, Connecticut*, New York: F.W. Beers, 1868, CSL.
20 "Bacon Academy and Congregational Church, Colchester," *Connecticut Historical Collections*, by John Warner Barber, New Haven: 1836; "The Reverend James W.C. Pennington," *The Underground Railroad in Connecticut*, by Horatio Strother, Middletown, CT: Wesleyan University Press, 1962; listing for Colored District School, *Geer's (late Gardner's) Hartford City Directory for 1842*, Hartford: 1842, GML.
21 Talcott Street Congregational Church, *Geer's Hartford City Directory for 1858-9*, Hartford: 1858, CHS; Amos Beman, Beman Collection, Yale Collection of American Literature, Beinecke Rare Book and Manuscript Library, Yale University, New Haven, Connecticut; "Southeastern view of the Wesleyan University, Middletown," *Connecticut Historical Collections*, by John Warner Barber, New Haven: 1836; list of black churches in New Haven, *Benham's City Directory and Annual Advertiser*, New Haven: 1847, GML.

CHAPTER EIGHT
The Voice of Conscience Grows Louder: Searching for Solutions to Slavery and Racism
22 *Injured Humanity: Being a Representation of What the Unhappy Children of Africa Endure from Those Who Call Themselves Christians*, broadside, illustrations by Alexander Anderson, New York: n.d., CHS; detail of map of the western coast of Africa, *A History of Africa*, by Samuel Griswold Goodrich. Louisville, KY: 1850, CHS.
23 "Wilbur Fisk," *The Life of Willbur Fisk, D.D.*, by Joseph Holdich, New York: 1842, GML; notice of Colonization Society meeting, *Connecticut Courant*, Oct. 19, 1819, CSL.

24 *The Liberator* masthead, May 7, 1831; *The Liberator*, January 1, 1831; detail of "A Declaration of the Sentiments of the People of Hartford, Regarding the Measures of the Abolitionists," 1835, CHS.

CHAPTER NINE
Seizing the Sword of Truth: Prudence Crandall Confounds Her Critics
26 William Lloyd Garrison, PCM; Arthur Tappan, Courtesy Oberlin College, from *Dictionary of America Portraits*, New York: Dover Publications, 1967.

CHAPTER TEN
Raging Bullies: The Battle of Canterbury Begins
27 James Forten, Historical Society of Pennsylvania (HSP), Leon Gardiner Collection; The Reverend Samuel May, PCM; Universalist Church, Brooklyn, Connecticut, PCM; ad for Canterbury Female Boarding School, *The Liberator*, March 2, 1833, PCM.
28 Andrew Judson, artist unknown, PCM; Catharine Esther Beecher, engraving by J.A.J. Wilcox, from *Dictionary of American Portraits*, New York: Dover Publications, 1967; Edward M. Jenks, account book, 1832-1872, CHS; "South view of the central part of Canterbury," *Connecticut Historical Collections*, by John Warner Barber, New Haven: 1836.
29 Samuel May House, Brooklyn, Connecticut, DRM.

CHAPTER ELEVEN
Adding Prosecution to Persecution: Using Old and New Laws to Close the Canterbury Female Boarding School
30 Pauper law, *Public Statute Laws of the State of Connecticut…1835*, Hartford: 1835; detail from *Barbarism*, broadside, 1833, CHS.
31 Detail of *Map of the United States*, by Eleazer Huntington, New York: E. Strong, 1835, CHS.
32 Connecticut State House on Staffordshire plate, by Ralph Stevenson, ca. 1815-1830, CHS; Senate Chamber, Old State House, Hartford, CHS, photograph by DRM.
33 "Black Law," *Public Statute Laws of the State of Connecticut … 1835*, Hartford: 1835.
34 Frontispiece, *Trial and Sketch of the Life of Oliver Watkins …*, Providence, RI; "North view of Brooklyn, (central part.)," *Connecticut Historical Collections*, by John Warner Barber, New Haven: 1836.
35 Packerville Baptist Church, Canterbury, Connecticut, DRM.
36 Portrait of Governor William W. Ellsworth, attributed to George F. Wright, MCH; window of courtroom in Windham County Court House (now Brooklyn Town Hall), DRM; George Benson house, Brooklyn, Connecticut, DRM; U.S. Constitution. Article IV, Section 2, *Public Statute Laws of the State of Connecticut…1835*, Hartford: 1835.
37 Portrait of Governor Chauncey Cleveland, by George F. Wright, MCH; silhouette of David Daggett, PCM; Staffordshire plate, England, PCM.
38 Old State House, Hartford, DRM.

CHAPTER TWELVE
When All Else Failed: Turning to the Tactics of Terror
39 Rev. Levi Kneeland gravestone, Packer Cemetery, Canterbury, Connecticut, DRM; Prudence Crandall house at night, PCM; "Colored Schools Broken Up, in the Free States," *Anti-Slavery Almanac*, 1839, PCM.
40 *The Liberator*, September 20, 1834; historical interpreter Kimberly Dysart in character as Prudence Crandall, at Prudence Crandall Museum, 2003, photograph by DRM.

CHAPTER THIRTEEN
In The Whirlwind's Wake: Exile, Tribulation, and Vindication
41 Francis Scott Key, from *Dictionary of America Portraits*, New York: Dover Publications, 1967; Troy, Illinois, PCM; Clarissa Cornell Crandall gravestone, Cornell-Munroe Cemetery, Plainfield, Connecticut, DRM.
42 Prudence Crandall house, Mendota, Illinois, PCM.
44 John Staples Smith gravestone, Cornell-Munroe Cemetery, Plainfield, Connecticut, DRM; Prudence Crandall, PCM.
45 Samuel Clemens, aka Mark Twain, circa 1886, PCM; Prudence Crandall house in Elk Falls, Kansas, PCM; Connecticut State Capitol, Hartford, constructed in 1878, DRM; Prudence Crandall gravestone, Elk Falls Cemetery, Elk Falls, Kansas, PCM.
46 Sarah Harris Fayerweather gravestone, Fernwood Cemetery, Kingston, Rhode Island, PCM; George and Sarah Harris Fayerweather house, Kingston, Rhode Island, PCM; Julia Williams Garnett obituary, *The Christian Recorder*, April 9, 1870.
47 Obituary, Harriet Rosette Lanson, *The Liberator*, April 6, 1836.

CHAPTER FOURTEEN
To All on Equal Terms: The Legacy of Prudence Crandall
48 Dred Scott, Courtesy New-York Historical Society, from *Dictionary of America Portraits*, New York: Dover Publications, 1967; Roger Brooke Taney, courtesy Library of Congress, from *Dictionary of American Portraits*, New York: Dover Publications, 1967.
49 "The American National Tree," courtesy of the National Constitution Center, Philadelphia, Pennsylvania, photographed by Scott Frances; *The Slave's Friend*, New York: American Anti-Slavery Society, 1836, from *Pictures and Stories from Forgotten Children's Books*, Dover Publications, 1969.

CHAPTER FIFTEEN
Sites in Eastern Connecticut Connected to the Prudence Crandall Episode
50 All photographs except Packerville Baptist Church and Brooklyn Unitarian Church, by DRM.
51 House of Charles and Mariah Davis Harris and house of William H. Harris, 30 and 34 Cedar Street, Norwich, Connecticut, DRM; Beulah Land Church of God in Christ, Norwich Female Academy, Norwich, Connecticut, DRM.

ACKNOWLEDGEMENTS OF PERMISSION TO QUOTE FROM MANUSCRIPTS

The Connecticut Historical Society, Hartford, Connecticut, manuscript collections:

12 Amy Baldwin to Mary Clark, [1833?], Baldwin Collection
30 Prudence Crandall to Rev. S.S. Jocelyn, April 17, 1833, typescript, original owned by Foster W. Rice
31 Prudence C. Philleo to [Ellen Larned], July 2, 1869, Hoadley Collection, Box 3, Men of Note

Yale University, New Haven, Connecticut, Beman Collection, Yale Collection of American Literature, Beinecke Rare Book and Manuscript Library:

21 Letter from anonymous Wesleyan University students to Amos Beman, October 5, 1833

SELECTED BIBLIOGRAPHY

Primary Sources

Report of the Arguments of Counsel, in the Case of Prudence Crandall, Plff. In Error, vs. State of Connecticut, Before the Supreme Court of Errors, at Their Session at Brooklyn, July Term, 1834, By a Member of the Bar. Boston: Garrison & Knapp, 1834.

A Statement of Facts, Respecting the School for Colored Females, in Canterbury, CT, Together with a Report of the Late Trial of Miss Prudence Crandall. Brooklyn, CT: Advertiser Press, 1833.

The Trial of Reuben Crandall, M.D., Charged with Publishing Seditious Libels, by Circulating the Publications of the American Anti-Slavery Society, Before the Circuit Court for the District of Columbia, Held at Washington, in April, 1836, Occupying the Court the Period of Ten Days. New-York: H.R. Piercy, 1836.

Secondary Sources

Clisby, Rena Keith. "Canterbury Pilgrims," 1947. Unpublished manuscript.

Cunningham, Jan. Jail Hill Historic District, National Register of Historic Places Registration Form, 1999.

Foote, Patrick. "Prudence Crandall's Canterbury, c. 1815-1835. The Bounds and Bonds of Rural New England Community in Fact and Fiction," 1995. Unpublished manuscript.

McCain, Diana Ross. "African-American Students Who Attended Prudence Crandall's Female Boarding School in Canterbury, Connecticut, April 1, 1833 – September 9, 1834," 2001. Unpublished research report prepared for the Connecticut Historical Commission.

Strane, Susan. *Whole-Souled Woman: Prudence Crandall and the Education of Black Women.* New York: W.W. Norton, 1990.

Welch, Marvis Olive. *Prudence Crandall: A Biography.* Manchester, CT: Jason Publishing, 1983.

White, David O. "Prudence Crandall," 1971. Unpublished manuscript.